NORTH KOREA

Flashpoints

The end of the Cold War unleashed a new era of international relations and accelerated the forces of globalization. Old conflicts reasserted themselves and the seeds of new threats were sown. This series examines those regions, relationships and issues that in the international arena have the potential to cause conflict between states. Each title offers a theoretically grounded analysis of the history, current complexion and likely outcome of the flashpoint to enrich our understanding of global politics, security and international relations.

Published

The Kurds: The Struggle for National Identity and Statehood
Mandana Hendessi

North Korea: Survival of a Political Dynasty
Ramon Pacheco Pardo

Taiwan: A Contested Democracy Under Threat
Jonathan Sullivan and Lev Nachman

NORTH KOREA

Survival of a Political Dynasty

Ramon Pacheco Pardo

agenda
publishing

First published in 2024 by Agenda Publishing

Agenda Publishing Limited
PO Box 185
Newcastle upon Tyne
NE20 2DH
www.agendapub.com

ISBN 978-1-78821-694-4 (hardcover)
ISBN 978-1-78821-695-1 (paperback)

British Library Cataloguing-in-Publication Data
A catalogue record for this book is available from the British Library

Typeset by JS Typesetting Ltd, Porthcawl, Mid Glamorgan
Printed and bound in the UK by CPI Group (UK) Ltd, Croydon, CR0 4YY

Contents

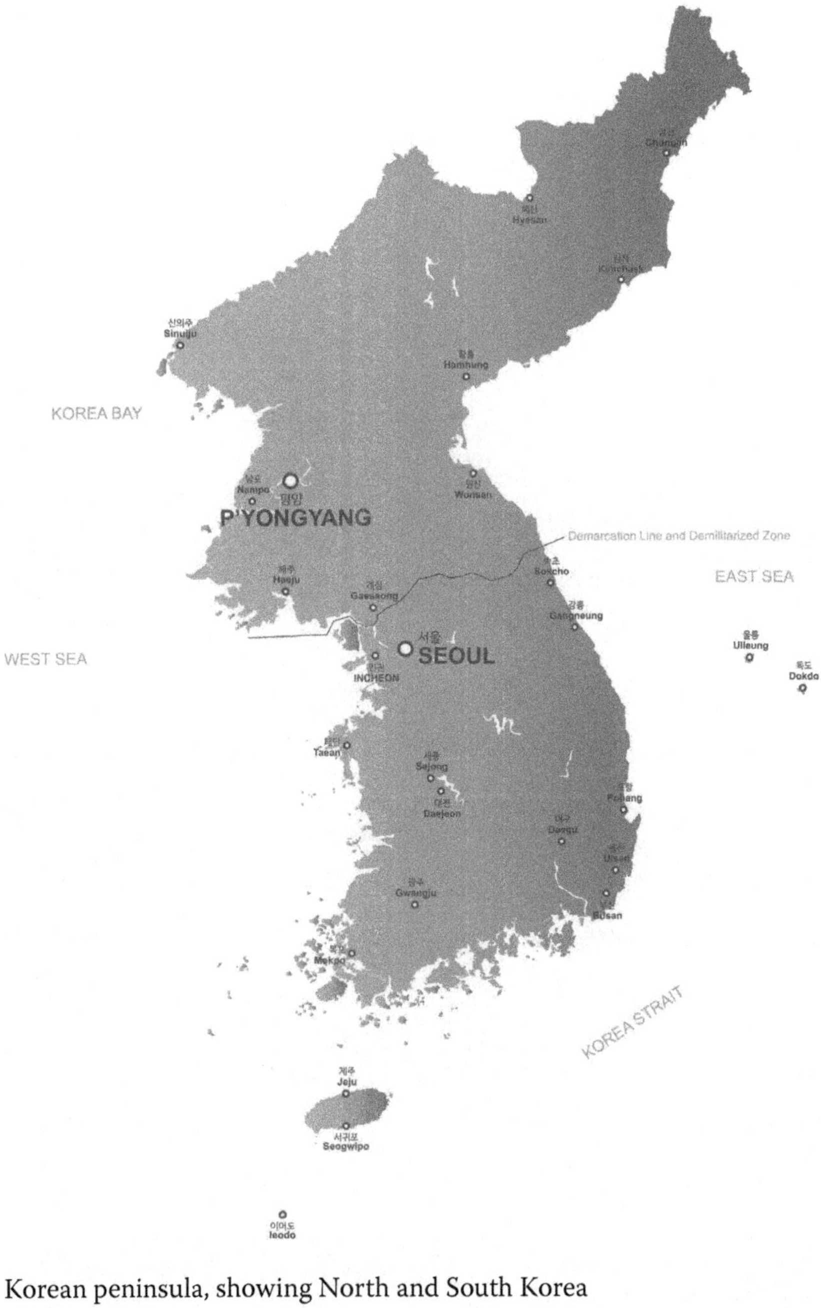

Korean peninsula, showing North and South Korea

Source: istock.

1

A brief history of Korea

The year was 1446. King Sejong the Great issued an official decree making *Hangul* the official alphabet for the Korean language. Sejong believed that using *Hangul*, as opposed to Classical Chinese, would increase the literacy rate among the general Korean population, especially the illiterate poor. Indeed, the alphabet's original name was *Hunminjeongeum*, or the Proper Sounds for the Instruction of the People, as opposed to *Hangul*, which means Great or Korean Script. The king himself had been involved in the development of the alphabet comprising a mere, fairly easy to remember 28 letters (at the time of writing only 24). Yet *Hangul* was disparaged by the Korean literati, who continued to use Chinese characters well into the twentieth century.

Eventually, *Hangul* would only be adopted for official documents in 1894. By then, it had become an expression of Korean *nationalism*. Forced to open by foreign powers including Japan, the United States and European countries, Koreans were divided between those seeking Japanese-style reform and those wishing to continue traditional Chinese-style economic and societal structures. But all Koreans agreed that they wanted the best for an independent Korea, with the late nineteenth century seeing the emergence of *minjok*: the idea of Korea's distinct ethnonationalism. Thus, King Gojong accepted *Hangul*, which Sejong had envisaged in the mid-fifteenth century as an instrument to educate the masses, as an instrument to differentiate Korea from China and Japan in the late nineteenth century.

This very brief account of the origins and officialization of *Hangul* as the Korean alphabet helps to illustrate Korea's history: a millennia-old sovereign country, surrounded by big powers and in constant need to assert its independence and distinctiveness from these same powers.

This conception of Korea and Korea's position in East Asia and across the world continues to inform the politics of the Korean Peninsula as of 2024, including North Korea's, where *Hangul* is in fact known as *Choson Muncha* or Korean Letters, an old term that emphasizes the Korean character of the alphabet.

THE ORIGINS OF KOREA

Legend has it that Korea was founded in 2333 BCE. Hwanin (the "Lord of Heaven") had a son, Hwanung, who eventually moved to earth to create his own kingdom.[1] A bear and a tiger wanted to live in Hwanung's kingdom, so they were offered a challenge. They would be able to become human and join Hwanung and his followers, but only if they could live 100 days in a cave with nothing but 20 cloves of garlic and a bundle of mugwort. The bear succeeded and became a woman known as Ungnyeo. Eventually, Hwanung transformed himself into a man and married Ungnyeo, who was longing for children. They gave birth to a son, Dangun Wanggeom, in the sacred Mount Paektu. Dangun then established Gojoseon (Old Joseon) in 2333 BCE. This legend is commemorated in both Koreas, as they celebrate Gaecheonjeol (National Foundation Day) every year in October.

While it is true that archaeologists have uncovered the remains of modern humans in the Korean Peninsula dating back to 30,000–40,000 years ago, the history of Korea as a unitary state can be traced back to the seventh century BCE. This is when several protostates formed a confederation called Gojoseon. The confederation disappeared following a military defeat at the hands of China's Han Empire in 108 BCE. The defeat was followed by centuries of division and confrontation throughout the Three Kingdoms period. Generally assumed to have lasted from 57 BCE to 668 CE, the three kingdoms of Goguryeo (later known as Goryeo), Silla and Baekjae occupied the Korean Peninsula, Manchuria and parts of what as of 2024 is modern Far East Russia. Arguably, these were the three first "modern" states in the Korean Peninsula, characterized by a

1 This section is adapted from Pacheco Pardo (2022) and Cha & Pacheco Pardo (2023).

hereditary monarchy, centralized armed forces, a fairly unified system of government and a modern culture.

The Northern and Southern States period followed from the Three Kingdoms era. From 668 to 935, Later Silla ruled over two-thirds of the Korean Peninsula. This kingdom is traditionally considered to be the birth of modern Korean culture. In particular, Gyeongju, its capital, saw the flourishing of buildings and art influenced by Buddhism and Confucianism that to this date help inform Korean culture. In the meantime, Goguryeo refugees founded Balhae in the northern part of the Korean Peninsula and parts of Manchuria. Balhae would last from 698 to 926 and established strong economic links with China. Internal divisions, however, resulted in the two kingdoms breaking down, and the Northern and Southern States period gave way to the Later Three Kingdoms period in 901, with Later Baekjae, Later Goguryeo and Later Silla fighting over the control of the Korean Peninsula and Balhae falling to the Liao dynasty.

In 936, King Taejo unified the Korean Peninsula. Taejo had established Goryeo (also spelled Koryo) in 918 to replace Later Goguryeo. Within 18 years, he led his country's army to victory over Later Baekje and Later Silla, while also moving to the north of the Korean Peninsula to conquer Balhae's older territories. This way, Taejo, or "Great Founder" (of Korea), established a kingdom that would rule the whole of the Korean Peninsula until 1392. This kingdom can be considered the first Korean kingdom. In fact, Taejo issued the Ten Injunctions in 943. This document established Goryeo as a separate entity from China, based on geographical location, their people's character and cultural identity. Taejo established Kaesong as the capital of Goryeo. Located towards the middle of the Korean Peninsula, a thousand years later Kaesong would become the venue of the biggest joint inter-Korean economic cooperation project.

The Goryeo period was marked by prosperity, relative peace and a cultural "Golden Age". The kingdom established strong economic relations with China, Liao-Khitan and Japan. At the same time, Goryeo institutionalized regular tribute missions to China. For centuries, the kingdom avoided major internal strife and repelled invasion attempts. Having said that, Goryeo became a vassal state of the Mongol Empire during 1270–1356, once the Mongols had been able to conquer China.

When it comes to culture, Buddhist monks and literati elites published the 6,000-chapter *Tripitaka Koreana* in the eleventh century. They also pioneered flexible moveable metal printing, publishing the *Sang-jong-ye-mun* (Goryeo Readings for Buddhist Ceremonies) in the twelfth century. The world's oldest surviving book using metal type printing was then published in Goryeo in 1377. This is the *Jikji* (Selected Teachings of Buddhist Sages and Zen Masters), after which UNESCO's Memory of the World Prize is named in commemoration.

THE JOSEON DYNASTY

The Joseon Dynasty, also known as the Yi Dynasty for its ruling family, was and to this date remains the longest period in Korean history.[2] From 1392 to 1910, the House of Yi ruled an independent Korea that periodically had to repel invasion attempts from China and Japan. Paradoxically, Joseon's history started following a decision by Goryeo to try to invade China. General Yi Seonggye was instructed to remove China's Ming Dynasty in 1388. Yi was opposed to this mission. Thus, he turned back once he reached the Amrok River that separates the Korean Peninsula from China. Upon reaching Kaesong, he launched a successful coup with the help of the many military leaders, aristocrats and regular citizens also opposed to Goryeo invading China. Yi then installed a puppet ruler while forcing the royal family to go into exile.

In 1392, Yi took the crown for himself and officially established Joseon. The name was inspired by Gojoseon, in an attempt by the House of Yi to link its reign to the mythical Dangun. Yi Seonggye himself took the title of Taejo of Joseon, thus clearly indicating that he was the founder of a new dynasty. To consolidate his rule and openly differentiate Joseon from Goryeo, Yi moved the capital to present-day Seoul in 1394. Then known as Hanyang, or formally Hanseong, the city could trace its modern origins to its time as the capital of Baekje in 18 BCE. Beyond the symbolism, the new capital had the advantage of lying next to the Han River, giving relatively easy access to China. Furthermore,

2 This section is adapted from Pacheco Pardo (2022) and Cha & Pacheco Pardo (2023).

Seoul/Hanyang is surrounded by four mountains, which made it easier to defend. Plus, its location meant that it had good *feng shui*, an important consideration for Yi.

The advent of the Joseon Dynasty meant the ascendance of Confucianism over Buddhism. Confucian scholars had supported the new king's coup, and they wanted their principles and thoughts to displace those that had been dominant during the Goryeo era. They were successful in their attempts to have their way of thinking dominate life during the Joseon period, to the extent that over time Joseon arguably became the most Confucian country in the world – even more so than China. This meant, above all, that government, society and, at least initially, the economy became hierarchical. When it came to government, it was organized into two main levels. At the central level, the Uijeongbu (State Council) was the highest organ of government. It was led by three officials whose main role was to advise the king on key state matters. The officials would then deliver the king's instructions to the ministers, who would lead their implementation. Meanwhile, at the regional level there were provincial governments, counties and districts.

Joseon society also became stratified. Land had been concentrated in the hands of a small number of high-level officials during the Goryeo period. King Taejo and his successors redistributed land among a greater number of aristocrats. The result was the emergence of the *yangban*. This was an aristocratic elite that held three types of power: political, for access to government was based on knowledge of Confucian texts that only the literati *yangban* could understand; economic, for the *yangban* ended up owning Joseon's land and could reap the benefits of this ownership; and culture, for the royal family and the *yangban* elite itself preferred and commissioned pieces of art including literature, paintings and sculptures produced by this class. Below the *yangban* were the *yangmin* or commoners, the *cheonmin* or base people, and the *nobi* or slaves. Often, one's birth family determined one's place in society. And almost always, one's gender determined one's position, for Confucianism prescribed that women should obey men – and the rules and regulations implemented by Joseon reflected this.

As for the economy of the Joseon era, the position of the *yangban* at the top endured throughout most of this period. The *yangban* extracted rent, labour and produce from their land, obtained the economic benefits that came from serving in government, received royal commissions and could afford to own *nobi*. Over time, however, a wealthy merchant class started to emerge. Comprising mainly *yangmin*, they included professionals working as peasants, fishermen, artisans or in marketplaces. And by the seventeenth century, the *jungin* or middle people emerged. They were workers with specialist knowledge who allowed the royal family and the *yangban* to be able to rule Joseon, either by filling specialized roles within the government bureaucracy or by providing their skills privately. Sometimes, the *jungin* were able to marry into the *yangban* class, particularly towards the end of the Joseon era when some social hierarchies started to loosen. It should be noted that, paradoxically, the economic role of women in the *yangban* class was more limited than in the other classes, because of the stricter adherence to Confucian principles among the upper classes.

Confucianism demanded that the people obeyed their rulers. But it also demanded that the rulers provided for the people. Thus, the House of Yi produced several kings who believed that their role was to improve the well-being of the Joseon population. It is in this context that Sejong the Great led the development of *Hangul*. At the time of writing, a 6.2 metre tall bronze statue of the king sits in front of Gyeongbokgung Palace in central Seoul. This was the palace that Joseon rulers inhabited for centuries. Furthermore, the King Sejong Institute is the organization in charge of spreading knowledge of the Korean language across the world. This attests to the importance of Joseon rulers providing for the people. Yet there were certainly Joseon rulers who did not live up to this principle and focused on extracting as much from the general population as possible.

In terms of foreign relations, Joseon continued to be China's tributary until the end of the nineteenth century. Whether this was because of a belief in Confucian principles of hierarchy or the result of a utilitarian approach to foreign relations, it is true that relations with China remained cordial for the most part. Instead, it was Japan that attempted to invade Joseon more frequently than China. Most notably, the Japanese navy attempted to land at the southern tip of the Korean Peninsula twice during the Imjin War of 1592–98. The invading navy was repelled by Admiral Yi Sunsin, arguably Korea's greatest war hero and honoured with a statue of his own in front of Sejong the Great's on the way to Gyeongbokgung Palace. In 1627 and 1636–37, the Manchus also attacked Joseon as they sought to have the House of Yi agree to their rule over China, which it finally did. This showed the limits of a tributary relation in safeguarding peace and prosperity in Joseon.

In the mid-nineteenth century, European powers and the United States arrived in Northeast Asia with the intention of incorporating the countries in the region into their colonial economies. China, Japan and Joseon were thus forced to open up their ports to the foreign invaders. Following the Meiji Restoration of 1868, Japan also joined Europe and the United States in demanding that China and Joseon open up. Japan also shifted its economic policy towards industrialization, in a process reminiscent of that followed by western Europe and the United States previously. And Japan also became an increasingly important military actor in its own right, defeating China in the First Sino–Japanese War of 1894–5 and Russia in the Russo–Japanese War of 1904–5. This dramatic change in the geopolitical situation of Northeast Asia resulted in a reconfiguration of Joseon's external relations, moving away from Sinocentrism and (formal) tributary status and towards a broader set of relations with the many countries seeking to get an economic and political foothold in the Korean Peninsula.

As change swept throughout Northeast Asia, internal debate and divisions took hold in Joseon. In 1860, Choe Je-u, a member of the *yangban* class, launched the Donghak (Eastern Learning) movement. Choe's goal was to create a society in which everyone was equal while rejecting Western influence. Two years later, a peasant revolt sought to spread Donghak across the country. Even though the revolt was quelled, there would be more uprisings during the remaining decades of the nineteenth century. Meanwhile, the Uijeongbu became divided between those *yangban* seeking to keep a traditional Confucian approach to government affairs and social mores, and those promoting social and economic reform to improve the lives of the other classes. Factionalism was not new to the Uijeongbu. But this time the divisions were about the very foundations of the system itself. Both groups agreed that they wanted Joseon to remain independent and the master of its own destiny. But they did not agree on whether adherence to tradition or embracing modernization was the best means to achieve this.

In the end, change became inevitable. In 1894, King Gojong approved the Gabo reform. Other than introducing *Hangul* instead of Chinese characters in official documents, as explained above, the reform put an end to slavery and therefore the *nobi* class, at least de jure, modified the system to access government posts by making it more open and meritocratic, and improved the situation of women by banning underage marriage and allowing widows to remarry. The Gabo reform was partially inspired by the Donghak movement, meaning that for the first time in centuries peasants were able to make their voices heard.

In 1897, three years after the Gabo reform and two years after Japan's victory in the First Sino–Japanese War, Gojong proclaimed the DaeHan Jeguk (Great Han Empire). Now Emperor Gojong, the Joseon ruler, continued with a reform programme through the Gwangmu Reform. The class system was formally abolished, an incipient land reform was launched, the education system was expanded and women gained more rights. At the same time, Joseon initiated an ambitious economic modernization programme, including the arrival of the tram and the train as well as incipient industrialization efforts. The reformers had the upper hand, and Korea seemed to be on a path to emulate Japan, Europe and the United States.

COLONIZATION BY AND LIBERATION FROM JAPAN[3]

Japan's ascendance at the turn of the twentieth century had a direct impact on Korea. From the perspective of Japanese leaders, control over Korea was necessary for three main reasons. First, Japan had always seen the Korean Peninsula as a dagger pointing towards its very heart; a dagger through which China and other Asian continental powers, now including Russia, could seek to pass on the way to launching a strike. Second, and conversely, the Korean Peninsula was the gateway for Japan to enter the Eurasian landmass on its way to Manchuria and influence over, if not outright territorial occupation of, Northeast Asia. Finally, and as colonial powers invariably do, Japan saw itself as a benign force

3 This section is adapted from Pacheco Pardo (2022) and Cha & Pacheco Pardo (2023).

that would bring "civilization" to the "backward" colonies that it hoped to acquire across Asia.

Japanese influence over Korea started to grow in the late nineteenth century, when Japanese diplomats, merchants and, eventually, soldiers began to arrive in the country and intervene in its politics. In fact, Japan forced Korea into its first unequal treaty, coercing it to open its ports and grant special rights to Japanese nationals, including extraterritoriality. This was the Ganghwa Treaty of 1876. Later on, Japanese agents assassinated Queen Min in 1895. Gojong's spouse, Min was one of the strongest advocates of Korea's independence from Japan. At the same time, Japanese diplomats pushed for reforms loosening ties between Korea and China, as well as removing the influence of the king/emperor and the *yangban* over the country's politics. In short, Japan started to lay the groundwork to take control of Korea.

Korea's fate was sealed following the Russo–Japanese War. To begin with, the United States and Japan signed the Taft–Katsura agreement shortly before the end of the war between Russia and Japan. With this document, Washington agreed to renounce any claim over Korea in exchange for Tokyo recognizing the United States' sphere of influence over the Philippines. Shortly afterwards, the Treaty of Portsmouth, whereby Japan and Russia agreed to put an end to their hostilities, "recognized" that Korea was part of Japan's sphere of influence. Shortly afterwards, Korea was forced to sign the Eulsa Treaty (Protectorate Treaty) with Japan in November 1905. The treaty effectively meant that Japan would annex Korea and take control of its foreign policy and trade.

Gojong tried to prevent the seemingly inevitable by sending a group of emissaries to the Hague Peace Conference where the big powers were seeking ways to prevent war among themselves as Italy, Germany, Japan and the United States joined the colonial race with older imperial powers such as Britain, France and the Netherlands. The emissaries were not even allowed into the room to present Korea's case. Gojong was forced to leave the throne, to be replaced by his son, Emperor Sunjong. Within three years, Sunjong was demoted to king within the Imperial House of Japan as Japan and Korea signed the annexation treaty that formally put the latter under the former's colonial rule.

August 1910 thus inaugurated one of the darkest periods in Korean history, with the country colonized by Japan until Tokyo's August 1945 surrender put an end to the Second World War in the Pacific. Japan's colonization started with a period of brutal repression lasting until roughly 1919. Japan centralized all power, with the Japanese governor-general essentially being granted total control over Korea. Japanese police and military forces launched a repression campaign, sending tens of thousands of Koreans to prison for illegal political activity and assembly. Many of those imprisoned were tortured, with Japan using some of the brutal methods for which it would become (in)famous during the Second World War. Thousands were also sentenced to death. This way, Japanese colonial forces ensured that any Korean who could have led an independence movement was either neutralized or had to go into exile. They were supported by Korean collaborators in their endeavours, as some Koreans either believed in or saw no option but to work together with their new rulers.

In addition, Japan launched a cadastral survey to confiscate and redistribute the land owned by the *yangban*. The colonial authorities presented this as an opportunity to divide the land among peasants. However, the process simply ensured that the colonial government itself would become the biggest landowner in the country, and that most land would be passed on to the many Japanese moving to Korea in search for better economic opportunities. The process thus proved traumatic for the *yangban*, many of whom saw their main source of income taken away, and to the peasants who either had to work for new Japanese landowners or who lost their jobs and had to migrate in search of better work prospects, either inside Korea itself or, as time went by, in Japan.

Furthermore, Japan's military and police forces successfully eliminated the Uibyeong (Righteous Armies) that had started to spread across Korea the previous decade to fight against Japan. Poorly equipped and with limited military training, the Uibyeong had nonetheless been able to mount a challenge to Japanese colonial rule while they had the implicit political support of Korea's rulers, as well as the economic support of sympathetic *yangban* and wealthy merchants. By the 1910s, these conditions were gone, while some Korean collaborators helped Japanese authorities to track the Uibyeong down. Thus, most independence fighters had to go into exile, mainly to Manchuria but eventually to other parts of China as Japan would eventually take control of this region in 1931 as well.

In order to ensure control over Korea and in preparation of imperial ambitions that extended over China, the Japanese government launched an infrastructure and education campaign. Korea's road, railroad and port network grew and was upgraded, as Japan sought to extract and transport minerals, foodstuffs, cotton and other produce from Korea for use in Japan itself or, eventually, in Manchuria and other territories occupied by Japan. Meanwhile, Japan also opened new schools and universities across the country, boosting student numbers, including women. The main goal was to educate Koreans in the idea that Japanese and Koreans were brothers and sisters, as well as to train young Koreans who would go on to serve the colonial authorities.

Certainly, opposition to Japan's colonial rule continued, especially as the occupation only encouraged the growth in the idea of *minjok*. Throughout the years, there were demonstrations, protests and other acts of resistance up and down the country. The biggest of them took place on 1 March 1919, which to this day is celebrated in both Koreas, especially in the South. The Sam-il (March 1st) Movement followed the death of Gojong, who was apparently poisoned, and was inspired by US President Woodrow Wilson's "Fourteen Points" declaration during the 1918 Paris Peace Conference to put an end to the First World War. Wilson had called for the right of self-determination of all people. On 1 March, Korean leaders read a declaration of independence in central Seoul and other parts of the country, demanding an end to Japan's colonial rule as a means to ensure Korea's self-determination. However, Japan's colonial authorities quickly repressed the movement, killing thousands of people while arresting tens of thousands more.

Even though the Sam-il Movement was unsuccessful in its main goal of securing Korea's independence, it was remarkable in that it was the first mass movement that united Koreans to demand their freedom. Political, religious and economic leaders joined hands with merchants, peasants and other groups. Men and women marched together and suffered the ensuing repression together. And in April, disparate groups were able to put ideological differences aside to launch the Provisional Government of the Republic of Korea in Shanghai. Led by Rhee Syngman, who would eventually become South Korea's first president, the government started to present Korea's interests internationally.

Meanwhile, the Sam-il Movement also taught the Japanese government that its heavy-handed approach to the rule of Korea was counterproductive. A new governor-general was appointed, and the colonial authorities removed some of the restrictions on the use of Korean that had been imposed and even allowed the publication of Korean-language newspapers. These included *Chosun Ilbo* and *Dong-A Ilbo,* which survive to this day. Furthermore, the 1920s were a period of global economic growth following the end of the First World War. Thus, Seoul, Pyongyang and other Korean cities witnessed a significant transformation, with new infrastructure, restaurants, cafes, theatres and cinemas. This was also a period in which Confucian structures were becoming looser, and women, in particular, started to have more freedoms than in the past. Overall, the 1920s were the least repressive years during Japan's colonization of Korea.

This period of relative loosening of repressive policies, however, was short-lived. In the 1930s, Japan was preparing for war, and occupied Korea was central to Japan's grand design to take control of Manchuria and other parts of China and, eventually, the rest of Asia. But the Japanese colonial authorities feared that Koreans would turn against them, especially in the context of slowing growth following the Wall Street financial crash of 1929. As a result, Japan launched a series of increasingly repressive policies following its invasion of Manchuria in 1931. As the years went by, it became clear that Japan's ultimate goal was to eliminate Korean identity.

Following Japan's Manchuria intervention, the Japanese government started to sanction sex slavery stations for its soldiers along the occupied territories. From 1932, tens of thousands of women from Korea, China and eventually Southeast Asia and Europe were forced into sexual slavery. Tens of thousands of women were raped multiple times each day by Japanese soldiers. Euphemistically called "comfort women", many of these women were killed by their captors, committed suicide or lost their minds. It would take decades after Korea's liberation for the first (South) Korean women to be able to publicly speak about their suffering.

Back in Korea, Japan issued the Rescript on Education in 1934. This banned the use of Korean in schools and other public offices while forcing Koreans to raise the Japanese flag, sing the Japanese national anthem and bow to the Japanese emperor on a daily basis. The objective was to inculcate the idea that Koreans were subjects of the Japanese emperor and had to forget about what made Korea distinct. In 1935, Japan passed the Shinto Shrine Order. This new edict made Shinto the official religion throughout Korea, with all Koreans ordered to worship Japan's main religion in school and public offices. Both Confucianism, still dominant among Koreans, and Christian thought, which had become increasingly popular across Korea from the late nineteenth century, were to be replaced by Shintoism.

In 1938, the Japanese authorities passed the National General Mobilization Law. As a result, around five million Koreans were conscripted into forced labour, with half a million of them being sent to Japan. Koreans were forced to work mainly in mines and factories, to support Japan's war effort. Tens or perhaps hundreds of thousands of them died because of harsh working conditions, accidents, malnutrition and illness. Japanese authorities saw the mobilized Koreans as plentiful labour that could be disposed of if necessary. Decades after the mobilization, (South) Korean workers and their descendants continued to demand reparations for their suffering.

That same year, the governor-general approved the *Naisen Ittai* (Japan-Korea One Body) report. It called for policies to finalize the assimilation of Koreans as subjects of the Japanese emperor. Thus, the colonial authorities passed the Soshi-kaimei (Name Order Edict) in 1940. This new piece of legislation forced all Koreans to adopt Japanese names, coercing them to give up their Korean names and, therefore, the greatest symbol of their Korean identity. Towards the end of the Second World War, over 80 per cent of Koreans officially had a Japanese name. By then, Korean had been completely eliminated from the school curriculum and all Korean-language newspapers had been closed. The only exception was the *Maeil Sinbo*, used for propaganda purposes.

At the same time, tens of thousands of Koreans joined the Japanese Imperial Army as it fought China and the United States, while occupying parts of Southeast Asia taken from European colonizers. Most had no choice but to join if they wanted to avoid forced labour, the death penalty or having another family member forced to join instead. Others were fooled into joining the army with the promise of some other job. Yet some Koreans joined the army of their colonial master for they thought that their country would never again regain independence.

They reasoned that it would be better to face the inevitable and serve the country that, back then, seemed destined to rule Korea and other parts of Asia for decades to come.

Differently, other Koreans joined the independence movement fighting against the Japanese in Manchuria, elsewhere in China and also inside Korea itself. Koreans from different ideologies fought next to each other, as well as with Chinese and Soviet soldiers. As the Second World War wore on and a Japanese defeat became first a possibility and then seemingly inevitable, more Koreans were encouraged to join the ranks of those who believed that Korea's freedom and independence was within reach. Among them, a young Kim Il-sung became a notable guerrilla leader. Japan even included Kim in its list of most wanted Korean fighters. In the future, Kim would leverage his role as an independence fighter as part of his cult of personality after he became the absolute leader of North Korea (see Chapter 2).

On 15 August 1945, Japanese Emperor Hirohito announced that Japan would surrender, thus putting an end to the Second World War. The news soon reached all corners of Korea, with Koreans of all ages, social classes and political ideologies celebrating as one. Exiled leaders, enslaved sex workers, suddenly demobilized soldiers and foreign-based independence fighters all started to flow back into Korea. The country was unrecognizable after 35 years as a colony, including over a decade serving Japan's war machine. But Koreans strongly believed that a brighter future awaited their country.

2

North Korea inside out

The date was 28 December 1955. Kim Il-sung delivered a speech: "On Eliminating Dogmatism and Formalism and Establishing Juche in Ideological Work" (Kim 1981). Where, and even exactly when, the speech was delivered remains subject to debate, such is the opacity and rewriting of history that is central to the way North Korea acts to this day. But the importance of the speech cannot be overstated. Kim criticized North Korea's rigid application of Soviet-style socialism, which he thought was unsuited to the domestic conditions that the only recently divided Korea was facing. At the time, the Workers' Party of Korea was already becoming divided between a pro-Soviet faction, a pro-Chinese faction, known as Yanan, and younger communists who were mainly pro-Korea and closer to Kim himself. The North Korean leader had avoided taking sides, until his speech of December 1955.

In his speech, Kim also introduced the idea of *Juche*, often translated as self-reliance. Even though the exact meaning of *Juche* wouldn't be laid out until decades later, introducing this term pointed to arguably the most important development in North Korean history: the idea that Kim himself was responsible for a new, nationalist ideology on which *his* rule would be based. Less than a decade after the division of Korea and following a disastrous attempt to reunify Korea by force, there were certainly many groups within North Korea who would have liked to remove Kim from power. The North Korean leader, however, did not seek to ingratiate himself with these groups, never mind share power. Following the speech, the Kim government engaged in a brutal purge campaign and launched the Chollima Movement, an industrialization programme that the regime made sure to link to Kim himself. From then on, it would be clear that the country and the leader were indivisible.

Almost 70 years after he introduced the concept of *Juche* in public for the first time, one of Kim Il-sung's grandsons rules North Korea. *Juche* continues to be Pyongyang's guiding ideology, at least in theory. And unlike all other communist regimes in history, North Korea has only been ruled by only one family espousing a single ideology that puts nationalism above all else. And, naturally from the Kim family's perspective, said family is the embodiment not only of the ideology but also of the North Korean state itself.

THE KIM FAMILY: THE ONLY HEREDITARY COMMUNIST DYNASTY IN HISTORY

The Kim family is arguably the most successful "political" family of the twentieth century and is still going strong in the twenty-first century. No other family has ruled a country for a longer period of time since the end of the Second World War. Yet there was no reason why this should have been the case. Kim Il-sung was certainly a war hero. Reportedly born as Kim Song-ju in 1912 in Mangyungbong, a small village near Pyongyang, Kim grew up in a Presbyterian family. Neither rich nor poor, the family may have lived a fairly unremarkable life were it not for Japan's occupation of Korea. Kim's family was active in the anti-Japanese occupation movement, and Kim had already became involved in anti-Japanese activities while a teenager. By his late teens, Kim had also become a Marxist, a movement then becoming increasingly attractive to Koreans opposed to both Japanese colonization and the Joseon-era stratification of Korean society. By the 1930s, Kim was leading one of several anti-Japanese guerrilla groups active in Manchuria, noted for his bravery and also his compassion. In 1935, him adopted the name Kim Il-sung: "Kim become the Sun". Supported by the Soviet Union and Chinese communist fighters, Kim would continue to fight against Japan until the very end of the Second World War in the Pacific (Suh 1995).

Following the end of the Second World War, the Soviet leader Josef Stalin wanted to make sure that his country would secure influence in the Korean Peninsula for itself. As such it agreed to the partition of Korea into two along the 38th parallel. Yet, and differently from the United States, the Soviet Union wanted to give the impression that it was allowing (North) Korea to rule itself, particularly after having helped Korea free itself from Japan's colonial rule. After a short search, Kim Il-sung became Stalin's preferred (North) Korean leader. After all, he had bona fide communist credentials, had fought with the Soviet forces during the Second World War and was well liked by those who had been under his command. Thus, Soviet forces transported Kim to Wonsan port close to the Soviet Union's Far East in September 1945. Two months later, Kim was installed as the First Secretary of the North Korean Branch Bureau of the Workers' Party of Korea. By February of the following year, he was named the leader of the Provisional People's Committee for North Korea. Essentially, he was the leader of the North, with the committee backed by Moscow. In the meantime, Kim secured the leadership of the Korean People's Army for himself (Suh 1995). By mid-1946, Kim was the de facto leader of the northern half of the Korean Peninsula, with the support of Stalin's Soviet Union and a home army. Certainly, these were formidable cards to play. Of course, Kim had his detractors. But a mixture of propaganda, his own popularity and repression did the rest, and Kim and his family have remained in power ever since.

Propaganda, certainly, is central to the Kim family's claim to be the natural leaders of North Korea. Above all, Kim Il-sung and his descendants claim to have the "Mount Paektu bloodline". This way, the Kims link their rule to Dangun, the mythical founder of Korea said to have been born in the mountain itself. Perhaps paradoxically, both Goryeo and Joseon rulers also considered the mountain to be sacred. Thus, the Kims are indirectly linking their rule to the two kingdoms that ensured Korea's history as a single entity, but which in theory North Korea is contrasted with because of their hierarchical nature. Furthermore, the Kims claim that Kim Jong-il was born in Mount Paektu itself, despite credible records that he was in fact born in the Soviet Union. And the North Korean Constitution declares that the mountain is "the sacred mountain of the revolution", a revolution of course led by Kim Il-sung and his descendants.[1]

---

1 The Socialist Constitution of the Democratic People's Republic of Korea. Pyongyang. 27 December 1972, last amended 29 August 2019.

Over time, propaganda has extended to grandiose buildings celebrating the Kims – especially Kim Il-sung – and media stories and posters exhorting the virtues of the North Korean revolution and attacking the United States, South Korea and Japan. With regard to the grandiose buildings, Pyongyang is home to the biggest stadium in the world: the Rungrado or May 1st Stadium, which was opened in 1989 and commemorates International Workers' Day, and can seat up to 150,000 spectators. It is home to lavish parades and displays to celebrate the Kim family. Furthermore, North Korea opened the impressive Arch of Triumph, the Tower of the Juche Idea and the Grand Study House of the People in 1982 to celebrate Kim Il-sung's 70th birthday. Also in the 1980s, the Kim regime sought to complete the 330-metre tall Ryugyong Hotel, at the time the tallest building in the Korean Peninsula and one of the tallest in Asia. In addition, Kim Il-sung and Kim Jong-il have their own 22-metre-tall bronze statues, the first erected in 1972 and the second in 2012 (Cha 2018).

As for media stories, it goes without saying that technically North Koreans only have access to state TV and radio stations plus newspapers, for the most part exhorting the virtues of life in North Korea under revolution and struggle, the suffering of South Koreans living under repressive regimes or the hostility of a United States bent on putting an end to the North Korean revolution. In addition, the country is littered with propaganda posters on these very same themes. Plus, more posters presenting the Kims as "men of the people" guiding their fellow North Koreans when not working hand in hand with them to improve the country's economy and society (Cha 2018). In this respect, the North Korea of 2024 continues in the tradition of communist regimes using propaganda to convince their citizens that their lives are really better than those of people living under capitalism.

Yet it cannot be denied that Kim Il-sung was a popular leader during his lifetime and beyond. There is a reason why he was named as the "Eternal President of the Democratic People's Republic of Korea" four years after his death. Kim Jong-il knew that this title would not only cement his father's legacy but also prop us his own rule by effectively placing it under the "eternal" guidance of his father. After all, Kim Il-sung was an independence hero who founded North Korea and, according to North Korean propaganda, defeated the "imperialist aggressors" from the United Stated during the Korean War. Furthermore, North Koreans who had lived under Japanese occupation did see their living standards improve under Kim Il-sung's rule, particularly in the period of rapid growth from the mid-1950s to the 1970s. And Kim was also able to maintain their country's independence, which could not be said of the House of Yi that had been unable to prevent colonization by Japan. Or South Korea, which according to North Korean propaganda is a "puppet" in the hands of its ally the United States (Suh 1995).

Kim Il-sung also proved to be a fairly popular leader in the communist and Non-Aligned Movement camps, which helped him to cement his role as the ruler of North Korea. From the 1950s to the 1980s, Kim travelled to the Soviet Union and China often. But he also toured East Germany, Hungary, Poland, Romania and other European countries in the communist camp. He also visited fellow Asian countries such as Indonesia, Mongolia and North Vietnam. And he visited Algeria and Mauritania in North Africa too. Kim was seen as a leader who had fought against and forced into negotiations none other than the ultimate "imperialist" power, the United States (Krishnan 1981). And compared to Japan or South Korea, he was leading North Korea's development without the need to host troops from any of the big powers. This was an appealing message to many leaders overseas but also at home.

Even as North Korea's economic situation worsened from the late 1970s onwards, Kim did not see his popularity decline. As older North Korean defectors have reported over the years, Kim was a good speaker and gave the impression of genuinely caring about his people. Thus, North Koreans shed genuine tears when Kim passed away in 1994 (Demick 2010). They had not known any other leader, and they were not yet aware of the backwardness of their country compared to South Korea or even China. Above all, Kim was the embodiment of North Korea as an independent country.

Yet propaganda and popularity would have been insufficient for Kim to maintain power when different elite groups thought that North Korea should follow a different path. So the North Korean leader followed the tried and tested methods of many a dictator: elite purges. Already following Korea's independence from Japan and Kim's arrival in Pyongyang, Kim purged members of the Provisional People's Committee for North Korea and other government bodies who were helping to set up the new state. Throughout the 1950s, both during and in the immediate aftermath of the Korean War, Kim purged communists and socialists with ties to the South as well as members of the pro-Soviet and Yanan factions. Korean People's Army leaders, whom Kim blamed for the failure of the Korean War to reunite the two Koreas, were also removed from power (Cha & Pacheco Pardo 2023). Not uncoincidentally, these purged army generals could have risen against Kim, who after all had ordered that North Korea invade the South.

Having said that, opposition to Kim's rule continued. So Kim acted even more decisively to remove anyone who could have challenged his position. Stalin died in 1953. His successor, Nikita Khrushchev, was moving the Soviet Union away from Stalinism and had no attachment to Kim (Szalontai 2005). This was not an auspicious situation for Kim. Sensing his weakness, the pro-Soviet and Yanan factions plotted to denounce Kim's rule at the plenum of the Central Committee of the Workers' Party of Korea due to take place after the 3rd Congress of the party, in 1956. When the plenum opened, leaders from the two factions duly denounced Kim. However, by then most members of the plenum were North Korean nationalists either appointed by Kim or who shared his view of an independent (North) Korea free from Soviet and Chinese influence. Kim easily withstood the denunciations of his rule, and within five years most members of the pro-Soviet and Yanan factions were either executed, imprisoned, in internal exile or expelled overseas (Cha & Pacheco Pardo 2023).

Kim still had to endure one more instance of a direct challenge to his rule. In 1966, the Kapsan Faction, including heroes and fighters from the anti-Japanese independence movement years, denounced Kim's cult of personality and proposed economic reforms. The faction also had a proposed leader with impeccable credentials: Pak Kum-chol, a war hero who had fought alongside Kim in the 1930s–1940s. Kim, however, launched a new elite purge campaign during the fifteenth plenum of the Central Committee of the Workers' Party of Korea of 1967. Kapsan Faction members were removed from power. Pak himself was sent to do factory work outside of Pyongyang. He was dead within weeks of the plenum (Cha 2018). Arguably, this was the last major challenge to Kim's rule. He was now free of credible internal challenges to his power. He was also free to designate his future successor.

Kim Jong-il, born to his father's first wife, Kim Jong-suk, was groomed to take office over decades. He joined the Workers' Party of Korea in 1961, and by 1967 he gave his first known speech to the party and was assigned his first official roles. He was only 26. But it was not clear that he would one day replace his father. Back then, it seemed that Kim Yong-ju, Kim Il-sung's younger brother, would one day become the leader of North Korea. In fact, Kim Yong-ju was his brother's envoy to secret talks with South Korea in 1972. This was the first time that the two Koreas had engaged in direct negotiations since the end of the Korean War. Kim Il-sung was thus showing the strong trust that he had in his brother. Yet Kim Jong-il was able to outmanoeuvre his uncle upon his appointment to the Central Committee of the Workers' Party of Korea in 1973. The party was engaged in ideological discussions about the merits of *Juche* as opposed to a more traditional interpretation of Marxism. Kim decisively supported the ideology introduced by his father. His uncle did not. After an internal struggle, Kim Jong-il emerged as his father's heir apparent. By 1980, his position was sealed and his uncle disappeared from public view.

Kim Jong-il, however, was not a popular leader, as many North Korean defectors have stated over the years (Demick 2010). To begin with, he was not a gifted orator and projected an image of being distant and detached. Furthermore, his rule started at the worst possible time. By 1994, North Korea was in the midst of its worst famine in decades. The "Arduous March" resulted in the deaths of hundreds of thousands of North Koreans because of malnourishment and preventable diseases. The famine was the result of economic mismanagement, the end of Soviet and Chinese economic support and natural disasters. But since it coincided with the passing away of Kim Il-sung, many North Koreans blamed their new leader, Kim Jong-il, for this turn of events (Demick 2010). On top of that, the younger Kim was no independence hero. Born towards the end of the Second World War, Kim did not have any military credentials to speak of. Once he passed away in late 2011, many North Koreans had to fake their tears for fear of being punished (Demick 2011).

Then along came Kim Jong-un. As with his father, Kim was not the obvious choice to take over the reins of the North Korean regime. His older half-brother, Kim Jong-nam, seemed to be the heir apparent until he was caught trying to enter Japan with a fake passport in 2001. Whether Kim Jong-un then became his father's heir apparent is unknown, for Jang Song-thaek, Kim's uncle via marriage to Kim Jong-il's sister, was also touted as North Korea's next leader. Yet Kim Jong-un was eventually able to replace his father at the helm of the North Korean regime (Pak 2020).

Virtually unknown until taking office, there were hopes that Kim would be a different type of leader as he had spent part of his schooling in Switzerland under an alias (Pak 2020). This turned out not to be the case. But perhaps recognizing the unpopularity of his father and, conversely, the enduring appeal of his grandfather, Kim consciously sought to take a leaf from his grandfather's book and present himself as a benevolent leader attentive to the interests of ordinary North Koreans (Fifield 2019). Whether his approach will work in the long run as it did for Kim Il-sung remains to be seen.

Interestingly, Kim has deviated from his grandfather and father in that he has sought to link his image to that of his wider family. In other words, he has presented himself as a "family man". Ri Sol-ju, Kim's wife, has made several public appearances with her husband over the years. Kim Ju-ae, Kim's young daughter, has also accompanied her father on public occasions, including missile tests. Kim Yo-jong, Kim's sister, who also spent time with him in Switzerland, has represented her brother and has official positions in the North Korean regime (Lee 2023). Kim Ju-ae and Kim Yo-jong, of course, would also have the Mount Paektu bloodline that the Kim family claims for itself.

At the same time, Kim Jong-un has not been able to rely on the lingering gratitude towards his grandfather that his father was able to build on. Furthermore, Kim took power in his late twenties in a country in which age and seniority are fundamental. Plus, the North Korean media only had a few months to present him as Kim Jong-il's designated successor, given his sudden death, whereas Kim himself was groomed for decades. In other words, the odds of Kim Jong-un being able to rule North Korea for over a decade were rather slim when he took office (Fifield 2019).

As a result, Kim launched an elite purge campaign unseen in North Korea since the 1950s–1960s. Most notably, Kim had his uncle Jang Song-thaek arrested during a politburo meeting of the Workers' Party of Korea in late 2013. Jang was allegedly too close to China for Kim's liking. His arrest was shown by North Korea's state broadcaster, Korean Central Television. This was unheard of in the history of North Korean purges. Thus, it was a clear and open statement by Kim that he would not hesitate to eliminate his opponents – including his own family members. Shortly after, Jang was savagely denounced by North Korean media and executed. Many other leaders close to Jang were also purged (Cha and Pacheco Pardo 2023).

In February 2017, Kim engaged in arguably North Korea's most daring assassination in decades. Kim Jong-nam, Kim's half-brother who had been living in Macau for years, was assassinated after an attack with VX nerve agent at Kuala Lumpur International Airport. Two women sprayed the agent on Kim Jong-nam's face. Fifteen minutes after the attack, he was dead. It turned out that the two women had been approached by North Korean agents and paid to carry out the attack, which they claimed they thought was a prank. Regardless of the circumstances of Kim Jong-nam's death, there was little doubt that the North Korean government was behind it (Pak 2020). Kim Jong-un, therefore, had no apparent challenger to his throne. As of 2024, he continues to rule as the third Kim in the Mount Paektu bloodline dynasty.

HIERARCHY UNDER COMMUNISM: A STRATIFIED AND MILITARIZED SOCIETY

"The Democratic People's Republic of Korea is an independent socialist state representing the interests of all the Korean People".[2] So reads article 1 of the North Korean Constitution. In short, North Korea self-describes as the true representative of an independent Korea, as opposed to South Korea, which is considered to be a US "puppet". Plus, North Korea also considers itself to be the representative of all Korean people living north and south of the 38th parallel. In this sense, North Korea does not differ from similar communist regimes – both past and present – that claim to serve the interests of their people.

2 The Socialist Constitution of the Democratic People's Republic of Korea.

This sits in contrast with the reality of North Korea: a communist dictatorship that is among the most repressive countries in the world (UN Human Rights Council 2014). The Supreme Leader is the de facto leader of the country and always a Kim: Kim Il-sung, Kim Jong-il and Kim Jong-un. Formally, power is shared among different bodies. Created in 2016, the State Affairs Commission headed by Kim Jong-un is the main administrative body. It replaced the National Defence Commission, the top institution from 1998 headed by Kim Jong-il. The General Secretary of the Workers' Party of Korea, for its part, leads the country's ruling party. The Kim in power has always held this role. Likewise, one of the Kims has held the title of Supreme Commander of the Korean People's Army since 1950, thus they are formally in control of the armed forces. To this we should add Kim Il-sung's title of "Eternal President", as explained above, and Kim Jong-il's titles of "Eternal Secretary General" and "Eternal Chairman" (of the National Defence Commission) since 2012, shortly after his death. And in 2016, the North Korean Constitution was amended to name Kim Il-sung and Kim Jong-il "eternal leaders of Juche Korea".[3] In short, the Kim family has always been in control of the different bodies of power in North Korea and has assigned the "eternal" rule of North Korea for itself. A rubber-stamp Supreme People's Assembly and a state-controlled judiciary are the two main bodies used to give the impression that there are some limits to the power that the Kims hold.

North Korea is, therefore, organized as a hierarchical political system with the Kims on top. The Standing Committee of the Supreme People's Assembly handles the day-to-day business of running the country, as per the decisions taken by the Kim that leads the country at any given time. The Supreme People's Assembly itself convenes once or twice a year (Ministry of Unification of the Republic of Korea 2017). In the case of the congresses of the Workers' Party of Korea, legally they should take place every five years. In practice, they have only been held when the Kims have so wanted. For example, there were four congresses in the period 1946–61, a fifth in 1970 and a sixth in 1980. Afterwards, there was a 36-year hiatus until the next congress. Kim Jong-il did not bother to convene even one while in power. Kim Jong-un convened the seventh congress in 2016 and the eighth one in 2021 (Han & Kim 2022).

3 *Ibid.*

So perhaps he will go by the law and hold them every five years. But he could very well decide that this will not be the case. And this is the point. The Kims take decisions and can also choose to what extent they pretend that they respect the structures and rules that, ultimately, they have decided for North Korea.

Arguably, this became clearest during the Kim Jong-il era. As just stated, Kim refrained from convening even a single Workers' Party Congress. But on top of that, he made clear that his would be a military rule. During his mandate, the National Defence Commission was the body that held ultimate power, as just explained. And arguably more importantly, throughout 1997–8 Kim put *Songun* or "military-first" as the driving force behind his government (Suh 2002). The Korean People's Army took a leading role in the economic governance and societal control policies of the country, to go together with its traditional role of protecting North Korea from foreign attacks. This way, Kim sidelined the Standing Committee of the Supreme People's Assembly, demoted the Workers' Party of Korea and installed the armed forces as the top institution in the country. In the context of the aftermath of the collapse of communist regimes across the world and the Arduous March that was only starting to end by then, it made sense for Kim to keep the armed forces happy while also using them to control any possible dissent. *Songun* would then be quietly shunned by Kim Jong-un, underscoring the extent to which each Kim can decide how to rule as they please.

The hierarchical nature of North Korea extends to the way in which society is organized. Dating back to the 1950s, the *songbun* system has been used to classify every single North Korean into one of three main groups and around 50 subgroups. In 1957, the decree "On the Transformation of the Struggle with Counterrevolutionary Elements into an All-People All-Party Movement" laid out how *songbun* works (Lankov 2002). Essentially, North Koreans are classified as core, wavering or basic, and hostile according to their family background going back three generations. The core includes independence fighters, revolutionaries against the previous societal system, and factory workers and peasants. The wavering or basic is made up of "ordinary" North Koreans, meaning those neither central to the narrative of the country about its struggle for independence or the structure of its economy nor opposed to the Kim regime. And the hostile includes landowners, religious leaders and pro-Japanese collaborators during colonial rule as well as pro-South Koreans during the Korean War. It is believed that approximately 20–30 per cent of North Koreans are part of the core, 50 per cent belong to the wavering or basic, and the remaining 20–30 per cent are classified as hostile, even though this is not known for sure. It is possible to move up or down the main groups and subgroups, but the direction is mainly down. A network of security and party officials observe every North Korean and take this decision (Lankov 2002). It should be stressed that one's classification is already decided at birth, for it is linked to family background. If one were to design a dystopian way to control society, this would be it. Paradoxically, therefore, *songbun* has more in common with Joseon's traditional way of organizing society than with any communist or socialist principle of all men and women being equal.

Songbun has certainly become weaker as the state's ability to provide for its own population has weakened, and eventually collapsed, while wealth and money have become more central to North Korean lives (see below). But *songbun* continues to determine access to the most desirable jobs and the best schools. And without a good *songbun*, no North Korean can aspire to the holy grail of the country's socio-economic life: permission to live in the capital, Pyongyang. For North Koreans are not free to choose where to live, and residence in Pyongyang is restricted (Kim 2020), with perhaps slightly more than three million North Koreans allowed to live in their country's capital out of a population estimated to stand at around 25 million people. In fact, one of the biggest punishments a North Korean can receive is to be exiled from Pyongyang to a smaller city or town elsewhere in the country (Thae 2024). Again, this is reminiscent of Joseon, when those who fell out of favour with the royal family would be sent to the countryside as punishment. Conversely, North Koreans aspire to receive official permission to move to Pyongyang whether for work or for study (Thae 2024). Such a move transforms one's life. Arguably, the only way up from Pyongyang is to be posted overseas as a diplomat or other official representative of the North Korean government. This allows one to see other countries, a possibility denied to the vast majority of North Koreans, and get access to foreign goods, many of which are not available in North Korea itself.

But the share of the population that can access this type of position is negligible.

North Korea's hierarchical societal structure has another key dividing line: gender. Traditional Confucian principles dictated that a wife should respect her husband, and if the husband passed away the eldest son became the head of the household. Differently from other communist countries in which the position of women vis-à-vis men improved, this was not the case in North Korea for decades. Women continued to be second to men in the eyes of the state. To an extent, the North Korean regime justified this state of affairs because it was men who led the work in the factories and fields that powered the North Korean economy. But there is no denying that centuries-old views of women were an even more important driver behind it. In fact, North Korea's rhetoric emphasized the role of women as wives and mothers for decades (Kim 2014). As a case in point, the wives of Kim Il-sung and Kim Jong-il had no public presence to speak of, which was a symbol of the position of women in society.

Yet the situation started to change as more women accessed professional jobs from the 1970s onwards, and especially since the Arduous March of the mid-1990s. The collapse of the central distribution system during that period meant that the state could not provide for its own population anymore. Thus, men working in government jobs were not able to feed their own families. In many households, women became the main breadwinners as they led the setting up of markets to buy and sell food and various goods. Money talks, even in North Korea (Kim 2014). So women putting food on the table brought a degree of equality that communism did not. As of 2024, Kim Jong-un's decision to surround himself with women symbolizes this change, even if all of them are family members or have impeccable *songbun*. Yet the improvement in the situation of women in North Korean society should not be exaggerated. The expectation is that they will continue to do most of the household chores, and formally they are often treated as secondary to their husbands. And as the 2023 Report of the UN Special Rapporteur on the situation of human rights in North Korea to the Human Rights Council stresses, sexual violence, domestic violence, arbitrary detention and discrimination are common (Office of the UN High Commissioner for Human Rights 2023). Plus, many women were trafficked to China for marriage against their will prior to the Covid-19 pandemic (Office of the UN High Commission for Human Rights 2023), before the North Korean regime closed the country's borders.

The Kim regime's use of human rights abuses and repression as a form of societal control is also part of life in North Korea within this context of a hierarchical structure of society. Mimicking the elite purges that the regime had engaged in over the decades, North Korea developed a sophisticated surveillance, prison and concentration camp system from the 1950s (UN Human Rights Council 2014). Arguably one of North Korea's greatest "success stories" has been the establishment of a repression system that has allowed the Kims' dictatorial regime to survive for over 75 years without any major challenges. Unlike the Soviet Union and other communist regimes that collapsed in the late 1980s and early 1990s, and unlike China that has suffered internal protests, most famously in Tiananmen Square in 1989, and unlike past dictatorships in places such as Latin America, North Africa and southern Europe, the Kim family has been able to maintain its rule.

North Korea has several concentration camps around the country, housing over 100,000 prisoners who endure hard labour, hunger or starvation and generally poor living conditions. Some of them house political prisoners accused of harbouring anti-Kim family or anti-North Korea sentiments. Others house criminals who for some arbitrary reason are sent to concentration camps rather than prisons. Executions by prison guards or by the armed forces are common. Plus, authorities can decide to send a whole family to a prison camp rather than the individual accused of a crime. There are also dozens of normal prisons across North Korea, with credible reports that detention can be fairly arbitrary and related to any sort of (alleged) crime, from listening to South Korean music to criticizing the Kim family to trading goods smuggled from China. Torture, beatings, rape and starvation are common (UN Human Rights Council 2014). In other words, North Koreans live in fear that those in a position of power may curtail their freedom for no particular reason. And those in a position of power also fear that those further up the hierarchy will do the same to them.

North Korea also is a militarized and militaristic society. To begin with, the Korean People's Army comprises an estimated 1.2 million active personnel. This makes it the fourth-biggest standing army in the world, only trailing the armies of China, India and the United States, which are much bigger countries in terms of population (International Institute for Strategic Studies 2023). North Korea also has an estimated 600,000 reserve personnel who are ready to mobilize in case of need (International Institute for Strategic Studies 2023). The size of the Korean People's Army means that approximately 5 per cent of the North Korean population is serving in the military at any given point in time, with a further 2.5 per cent in reserve. Plus, it is estimated that the North Korean government spends up to 25 per cent of its annual budget on its military capabilities (International Institute for Strategic Studies 2023). This clearly shows the importance that the Kim family attaches to the military. Even as North Korea remains poor and hundreds of thousands of North Koreans have limited access to food and other goods, the North Korean regime ensures that the armed forces are well funded. The Kims have learnt the value of having a military that represses its own population and, equally relevant, refrains from launching a coup to remove the dictator in power.

The Korean People's Army is not just the country's armed forces. It also plays a central role in the economy of North Korea. The army runs businesses, supports construction and building work, and grows and helps to distribute food (Tertitskiy 2023). The army also engages in export–import activities, including along the borders with China and Russia (Tertitskiy 2023). Furthermore, army personnel are involved in North Korea's cyber activities such as hacking, from which the North Korean government gets much of its income (Tertitskiy 2023). In addition, the army is in charge of border control and extracts bribes from traders moving in and out of China (Tertitskiy 2023). Even though the heyday of the Korean People's Army was during the *Songun* years under Kim Jong-il, its economic role both preceded and has continued after his time as leader of the country. In other words, the Korean People's Army is central to the running of the North Korean economy, whether official, state-run economic activities or (nominally) underground, market-led economic exchanges.

The militarization of North Korean life is also the result of universal male conscription. All North Korean men have to enlist in the armed forces upon graduation at the age of 17 or 18, reportedly serving for up to ten years. Furthermore, reportedly all North Korean women are also conscripted since a decree approved in 2015. Before, only a select number of women were conscripted (Mohan 2017). Mandatory conscription means that every North Korean will have experience serving in the military at some point. Certainly, being ready to defend the country against a possible attack from the United States and South Korea is a key reason behind mandatory conscription. But at the same time, conscription serves as a mechanism of social and ideological control. North Koreans do not have many rights under normal circumstances, but they have even less during their military service.

North Korea is also home to the Worker-Peasant Red Guard. Dating back to 1959, this is a paramilitary organization entrusted with national security, including crowd control, border security, reconstruction work and natural disaster response. It comprises men and women from the age of 17 onwards. In addition, there is also a youth wing: the Red Youth Guard. Established by Kim Il-sung in 1970, the Red Youth Guard operates across schools. Male and female middle and high school students have to attend mandatory training on Saturdays. Millions of North Koreans serve in the red guards (Young 2021b). They can also be mobilized in case of confrontation with the United Sates or South Korea, and in fact there are units trained in the use of some types of arms. This way, North Koreans are constantly reminded that theirs is a society with military power at the centre of everyday life.

Arguably, the Korean People's Army and related organizations are some of the few institutions that did not collapse following the end of the Cold War and the Arduous March in the 1990s. The central distribution system never recovered from those years. The operation of factories is patchy because of the poor state of the North Korean economy, including unreliable access to electricity and materials. Likewise, peasant cooperatives have become less central to North Korean life as access to fertilizers and tools has become more difficult. Membership of the Workers' Party of Korea is restricted, never mind the Supreme People's Assembly and other government institutions. But the military has continued to operate, seemingly unaffected by the vicissitudes the country has faced. Certainly, conditions are not as good as in the armed forces of richer countries, starting with South Korea, North Korea's main "enemy". North Korean troops have to grow their own food to supplement relatively small rations, often have to fix their own barracks and vehicles when they break down and have limited uniforms and equipment (Tertitskiy 2023). Yet the army has continued to function even in times of hardship, and there is no indication that it has sought to overhaul the North Korean system or launch a coup against the Kim family.

THE ECONOMY: SELF-RELIANT, BENEFACTOR-DEPENDENT OR SIMPLY FAILED?

North Korea is located in Northeast Asia. This is one of the richest regions in the world, home to 4 of the 20 largest economies globally: China, Japan, South Korea and Taiwan. Of these, China is predicted to challenge the United States for the title of biggest economy in the world in the coming years, and Japan, South Korea and Taiwan are fully developed, high-tech economies. In addition, North Korea shares a border not only with China but also with Russia, one of the 15 largest economies globally. Together with North America and western Europe, Northeast Asia is the richest region in the world. If there is a region of the world in which any developing country would like to be based, Northeast Asia would surely be at the top of the list of preferences.

North Korea, however, is a poor country. Its estimated nominal gross domestic product (GDP) per capita is US$640. This is the second lowest in the whole of Asia, only above an Afghanistan suffering from decades of instability and conflict and even below Yemen, which at the time of writing is engulfed in a civil war dating back to 2014. South Korea's GDP is over 50 times bigger than the North's (Maddison Project 2022). In fact, North Korea's GDP per capita as of 2022 was at the level of South Korea's in the mid-1970s (Maddison Project 2022). This in spite of the economy of the two Koreas being roughly the same size following the Korean War. The World Food Programme, which has been operating in North Korea since the 1990s and has an office in Pyongyang, reports that 10.7 million North Koreans are undernourished: over 40 per cent of the country's population. And the situation is only getting worse, with 18 per cent of children stunted because of malnutrition (World Food Programme 2023a).[4]

4 All these data were collected prior to the Covid-19 pandemic. In common with other aid agencies, most foreign embassies and non-governmental

Even though Koreans on both sides of the 38th parallel are genetically the same people, younger North Koreans are noticeably shorter than their South Korean cousins because of their different diets and access to food and modern health care. This can be easily observed in the Korean Demilitarized Zone (DMZ) where North and South Korean soldiers face each other. Presumably, North Korea sends its fittest and tallest soldiers to the only area in which they encounter their South Korean counterparts and tourist groups on a daily basis. And yet, they are dwarfed by the (much) taller South Korean soldiers.

There is no other way of putting it: from an economic perspective, North Korea is a failed state. It makes the news because of the Kim family, nuclear and missile tests, threats of war, verbal tirades against South Korea and the United States or human rights violations. But its dire economic situation, inability to feed its own population and general economic backwardness while sitting in the middle of one of the richest regions in the world should be as newsworthy. Especially considering that back in the 1950s North Korea was in a better position than the South to develop, since it is a mineral-rich country and Japan had developed its infrastructure and hydroelectric power-generation plants during the colonial period as a way to support its expansion into Manchuria.

How did North Korea reach this point? Arguably, North Korea is a textbook example of how poor economic planning and policy-making cannot be offset regardless of a country's resources. North Korea nationalized key industries during the second half of the 1940s and also launched a land reform process as lands formerly owned by Japanese colonizers were left vacant (Cumings 2005). This seemed like sensible measures for a newly independent yet poor country recovering from years of brutal occupation in which its economy had been oriented towards supporting the colonial power. But Kim Il-sung's decision to invade South Korea put an end to these reforms. Plus, the war resulted in the destruction of a large proportion of North Korean infrastructure – including as a result of a carpet-bombing campaign by the US air forces – and the death of hundreds of thousands of (potential) workers

---

organizations, the World Food Programme's office in Pyongyang had to close during the pandemic and its foreign personnel left the country.

who could have helped build the economic foundations of the country (Cumings 2005).

Following the war, the Kim Il-sung regime launched its plan to develop a communist-style centralized economy in earnest. The key objective was threefold. First, and most obviously, Kim wanted to develop the economy of North Korea as a way to move beyond the poverty of the colonial era and improve the well-being of the country's population. Second, the North Korean leader was engaged in a de facto competition with the South and needed to prove that the North's economic management strategy was more successful. And third, Kim wanted to ensure that North Korea became economically strong so as to assert its independence from third parties, including the Soviet Union and China, which were already starting to compete for the leadership of the communist camp.

To this end, North Korea first launched a three-year reconstruction plan in 1954. The main objective was to rebuild the economy of the country after the three years of the Korean War. The top two priorities were to lay the groundwork to develop heavy industry, a sector that Japan had started to develop during the colonial years but that mostly laid in ruins after the bombing by the American air forces during the war, and to collectivize the agricultural and farming sector along communist precepts. The Soviet Union, China and central and eastern European countries, including Czechoslovakia, East Germany and Poland, provided funding, materials and expertise to help North Korea in its reconstruction efforts (Pacheco Pardo 2021a). The reconstruction plan made sense for Kim both from an ideological and a material perspective, and North Korea was on track to reach pre-war output levels as the plan drew to a close.

Yet this is when North Korea's economic planning problems started to emerge, even if they would take two decades to manifest themselves. In 1955, as stated above, Kim Il-sung had presented his idea of *Juche*. It would be a few years before the idea took shape, but it pointed towards Kim's goal of self-reliance, including in the economy. In 1956, Kim presented the Cheollima Movement. The *cheollima* is a mythical flying horse that, according to legend, can travel up to 500 kilometres per day. The country was plastered with Cheollima Movement propaganda posters. The "Riders of the *Cheollima*", or workers who exceeded their production quotas as set by their managers following from government guidelines, became examples for the rest of society (Cha 2018). Following the Korean War and postwar reconstruction period, Kim wanted to energize the North Korean workers to work harder and produce more for the sake of the North Korean state. The idea made sense in the context of a poor economy in competition with the South. But the results of the Cheollima Movement were short-term gains at the expense of long-term viability, along with exhausted workers who were constantly asked to do more. Coming shortly after the Korean War and Japanese colonization, the Cheollima Movement probably did not make North Koreans feel that they had been liberated from decades of oppression and violence.

In 1957, North Korea launched a Five-Year Plan based upon the spirit of the Cheollima Movement. The focus continued to be the development of a heavy industry and agricultural collectivization. The latter was fully achieved during this period. The former, however, was not. The Soviet Union and other countries in the communist bloc reduced their support to North Korea, partly to focus on their own economic development and partly because Pyongyang wanted to reduce reliance on foreign countries. Without their support, North Korea started to suffer from building material shortages and deficits in expertise. Furthermore, individual workers, firms and factories were effectively competing against each other as they sought to meet their production quotas in spite of these shortages. As a result, corruption started to cripple the economy as well-connected managers and factories pushed to get access to the materials and expertise that they needed (Cha and Pacheco Pardo 2023). Rather than promoting a sense of collectivization and cooperation, the reality was that mistrust and competition started to take over.

Still, North Korea's economic growth and GDP per capita exceeded South Korea's during these years. With more limited natural resources, its infrastructure also destroyed by the war, and facing internal divisions and protests, South Korea was taking longer to recover. Its leader, Rhee Syngman, was focusing on education, vaccination and infrastructure building. These would eventually be beneficial for long-term, sustainable economic growth. But he seemed to have no short-term economic plan beyond reliance on aid coming from the United States, and the state of the economy was so parlous that he was forced into exile as a result of his regime's corruption and authoritarianism. In contrast, at least the North had political stability and, seemingly, a clear path to promote long-term growth.

From the 1960s, however, the North Korean economy started to take a turn for the worse. Agricultural collectivization and Kim's insistence on *Juche* resulted in some instances of food shortages. Collective farms were unable to meet their quotas as manpower was moved to the industrial sector, while Pyongyang was seeking to reduce food imports from overseas (even if North Korea was only able to feed its population thanks to food transfers, especially from China). Meanwhile, the focus on heavy industry was not necessarily well suited for an economy the size of North Korea's at the same time as the country was seeking to increase self-reliance. Thus, Pyongyang's Seven-Year Plan, launched in 1961, had to be extended by three years as North Korea failed to meet its own targets. The Six-Year Plan launched in 1971 supposedly met its targets (Yang 2015). But by then North Korea's statistics were either non-existent or unreliable depending on the sector, so it was not possible to know whether this was the case. Perhaps a more useful way to gauge the true state of the North Korean economy throughout this period was the fact that South Korea's economic growth rates were exceeding the North's.

Furthermore, North Korea had its first debt crisis during this period of time. In order to fulfil its ambitious targets, the Kim regime went on a shopping spree. North Korea bought machinery and equipment from northern European countries such as Finland and Sweden. Meanwhile, western European countries such as France and the United Kingdom plus Japan provided credit to North Korea to build fertilizer and cement plants, among other things. However, North Korea was unable to fully pay for its purchases, since it was not able to scale up capacity to the level required to generate the money to do so. North Korea's inability to repay its debt was another sign of its economic weakness. (In fact, as of 2024 North Korea is yet to repay Finland and Sweden.)

By the 1980s, it had become clear that the North Korean economy was in trouble. The Seven-Year Plans of 1978 and 1987 went unfulfilled, with the first one extended beyond its initial period as it was clear that its goals had not been met. The centralized distribution system had started to fail, and by the 1980s not all North Koreans were receiving three meals a day (Cha 2018). In the meantime, the Kim family diverted scarce resources to the building of the megalomaniac monuments celebrating itself described earlier. It also invested between US$4 billion and US$9 billion to build around 260 facilities to host the 13th Festival of Youth and Students (Cha 2018). Hosted in Pyongyang in 1989 as a response to the Seoul Olympic Games of 1988, this was an unnecessary extravaganza that left North Korea bankrupt. In the meantime, North Korea continued to receive food transfers from its fellow communist countries, mainly China and the Soviet Union. The government also introduced some market reforms to attract foreign investment, following in the steps of Deng Xiaoping's China. These were unsuccessful in the case of North Korea though, given its smaller size and unreliable legal system (Yang 2015). Thus, it was becoming ever more difficult to hide the poor state of its economy. As a case in point, North Korea decided to provide relief aid to South Korea in 1984, following severe flooding that affected Seoul and two other provinces. This was the first time that the South had agreed to receive aid from the North. However, South Koreans were shocked at the poor quality of the rice, fabric and medicines provided by the North (KBS World 2018). They were able to see first-hand how much more advanced their country had become. If they still harboured any doubts that their economy was stronger and more modern than the North's, this act of generosity from the Kim Il-sung regime eliminated any lingering doubts.

The final shock to the North Korean economy came with the collapse of the Soviet Union and the communist camp in the late 1980s and early 1990s. In spite of repeated calls for self-reliance, the truth was that the North Korean economy was dependent on the Soviet Union and China to function. In fact, it had arguably been Kim's ability to play Moscow against Beijing that had allowed the North Korean economy to survive (Pacheco Pardo 2019). In 1991, however, the Soviet Union disintegrated and it stopped food and fuel shipments to North Korea. Shortly after, China started to demand that North Korea pay market prices for its imports, as opposed to receiving them for free or at special, communist bloc rates. Pyongyang was unable to pay these prices (Oh & Hassig 2000). In 1992, the government was forced to launch the "Let's Eat Two Meals per Day Campaign" (Oh & Hassig 2000). Essentially, an admission that the government was unable to feed its own population.

The structure of the North Korean economy was transformed during the Arduous March. The centralized distribution system collapsed and human ingenuity took hold. Ordinary North Koreans took to the countryside, mountains and rivers for food and firewood. And amid unspeakable suffering, with hundreds of thousands of people starving to death, markets started to pop up across the country. China, Japan, South Korea and the United States were among the many countries that started to provide food, medicines and other aid to North Korea as its population faced famine and destitution. Entrepreneurial North Koreans started to cross over to China to cover their basic necessities and eventually other products as well. Thus, North Koreans started to trade in goods and services in these markets (Kim 2014).

The *jangmadang* or markets that spread from the mid-1990s onwards are, as of 2024, the bread and butter of the modern North Korean economy. At first, the Kim Jong-il regime tried to crack down on them once the worst of the Arduous March was over. However, Kim agreed to market reforms in July 2002 reminiscent of those pursued by China from the late 1970s and Vietnam from the 1990s. Among others, markets were allowed and public salaries became performance-related (Kim 2017). It was an admission that there was little that the state could do to stop North Korea's incipient market economy. As the border with China became more porous, North Koreans started to have access to mobile phones, TV sets, pianos and other products that their country was unable to produce. They also started to have access to South Korean and Chinese movies, dramas and pop music, which proved more popular than domestic productions (Kim 2017). By 2018, there were at least 436 officially sanctioned markets in North Korea (CSIS 2018). And the *donju*, or masters of money, had become a new wealthy class who had made their money mainly in the *jangmadang*.

In my conversations with North Korean officials and defectors in late 2019 across Europe, they recounted how these markets operated in the capital Pyongyang and other parts of the country. They explained that some traders specialized in particular products, say clothes, beauty products or electronics. One would generally have to haggle, but for the most part prices fluctuated within fairly narrow bands. Payment could be made in different currencies, and in fact foreign currencies such as US dollars were often preferred. One could also order particular goods and traders would try to procure them. Many markets were not open to foreigners, but some were and diplomats, aid workers or tourists could venture into them. Former European diplomats who have been based in North Korea also corroborated this last point in conversations with the author held throughout 2020. In other words, the *jangmadang* were, for the most part, unremarkable and similar to markets elsewhere in the world. This is worth noting because the assumption is that North Korea lacks such places. But the reality is that the country has had to adapt to the failures of its communist-style economy.

The result of these changes is that the North Korean economy mixes central planning and market elements as of 2024. Kim Jong-un has tried to reinforce the former, most notably by launching a Five-Year Plan in 2016, North Korea's first since the 1980s (Fifield 2016). Plus, Kim has also launched a building spree to improve North Korea's infrastructure and housing. At the same time, Kim has sometimes cracked down on markets, as his father did, but for the most part they have continued to operate relatively free of government interference. In fact, Kim announced the launch of his *byungjin* line at the Korean Workers' Party meeting of March 2013. This refers to the parallel development of nuclear weapons and the economy (KCNA 2013a). Compared to his father, Kim Jong-un has become more open about the need to improve the North Korean economy.

However, North Korea continues to be a poor country. The decades-old economic mismanagement of the Kim family cannot be resolved in a few years. Furthermore, North Korea's economy is among the most heavily sanctioned in the world as a result of the nuclear and missile programme pursued by Pyongyang (UN Security Council 2023b). This calls into question the extent to which Kim Jong-un prioritizes economic development. And North Korea was the first country to shut down its borders at the start of the Covid-19 pandemic, even before China, and still in 2023 was yet to fully reopen (Smith & Kiyada 2023). This has resulted in another economic hit.

North Korea is also highly dependent on trade with China for its economic survival. North Korea's neighbour accounts for around 90 per cent of its total trade and a large share of foreign investment (Kim 2017). Without the economic lifeline provided by China, and to an extent by Russia, the North Korean economy could again suffer a catastrophic crisis. In sharp contrast to the ideal of *Juche*, the North Korea of 2024 heavily relies on its main benefactor. For North Korea to change this reality, the Kim family would need to take a bold decision to truly transform the economy of the country it has ruled since the beginning.

3

Relations with the USA

It was a sunny morning in Singapore. US President Donald Trump arrived at the luxury Capella Resort located in Sentosa, an island off the southern coast of the Southeast Asian country. A few minutes later, North Korean leader Kim Jong-un arrived at the same spot. Twelve flags, six American and six North Korean, were neatly lined up by the entrance to one of the resort's buildings. Trump walked in from the right. Kim did the same from the left. The two leaders met right in the middle of the set of flags and shook hands for 12 seconds as the photo cameras from selected media clicked incessantly. Trump and Kim exchanged pleasantries, and then left by the side from which Kim had arrived, followed by their respective interpreters right behind. The date was 12 June 2018. The local time was 9.05 am. The first summit between a sitting US president and his North Korean counterpart had begun.

The two leaders held a one-on-one meeting, with only their interpreters in attendance. This was followed by a meeting between the American and North Korean delegations, extending into a working lunch. Trump and Kim then issued a joint statement calling for new bilateral relations between their two countries, peace on the Korean Peninsula, the denuclearization of North Korea and the repatriation of US prisoner of war/missing in action remains by North Korea. This was not exactly path-breaking, for previous agreements between Washington and Pyongyang had already called for similar measures. But the order mattered: new bilateral relations and peace were listed before denuclearization. This was a diplomatic victory for Kim, for the United States remains North Korea's sworn enemy on paper. Its very existence and "threat" to the existence of North Korea in its current form is the main reason that Pyongyang gives to explain the development of its nuclear programme.

Yet at the same time North Korea craves recognition from the United States, which it sees as the key to unlocking its economic development and international status. Indeed, North Korea is one of only a handful of countries yet to have diplomatic relations with the United States as of 2024; a failure for the Kim family that the 2018 Singapore Summit did not help reverse.

Over 75 years after North Korea became an independent country, its relations with the United States thus continue to be marked by hostility. North Korea's official media denounce the US government, military or foreign policy on a daily basis. The country's leaders regularly do the same. The alleged threat that the United States may strike North Korea justifies or serves as an excuse, depending on one's view, for the Kim family's prioritization of weapons over the well-being of the North Korean population. But the Kim family also knows that achieving diplomatic relations with Washington would be the ultimate recognition of its rule over North Korea, which is why Kim Jong-un continues to strive for the goal that has eluded the Kims for decades.

PUBLIC ENEMY NUMBER ONE: THE UNITED STATES

The roots of North Korea's hostility and resentment towards the United States can be traced back to Korea's postcolonial years. It was two US army officers who artificially divided the Korean Peninsula along the 38th parallel to ensure that Soviet armed forces would not take control of the whole of Korea, as Japanese troops and civilians withdrew while the US army attempted to reach the country as quickly as possible to prevent a communist takeover. The division ensured that Seoul, Korea's capital city throughout the Joseon Dynasty, remained below the 38th parallel. Thus, the Soviet army made Pyongyang the temporary capital of the northern half upon reaching Korea in August 1945. North Korea would then make it the country's capital upon its establishment in 1948. But from a North Korean perspective, this was an unnatural state of affairs that only resulted from decisions taken by US officials on the other side of the Pacific Ocean with no knowledge of the history of Korea.

North Korea's grievances against the United States were set in stone during this period. To begin with, some leaders from North and South

Korea sought to accelerate the end of the de facto division between their two countries. However, neither the Soviet Union nor the United States wanted to abandon their spheres of influence. The Korean Peninsula had been the bridge that Japan had used to invade Manchuria. With Japan occupied by the United States and the communist camp about to expel the nationalist forces from mainland China as the Chinese Civil War drew to a close, the Korean Peninsula was becoming a key battleground of the incipient Cold War (Cha & Pacheco Pardo 2023). Thus, the United States Army Military Government in Korea (USAMGIK), established in the southern half of the Korean Peninsula in September 1945, worked to eliminate any communist influence. This included support for avowed anti-communist leader Rhee Syngman, material and political support for the southern police force and army to persecute and imprison communist sympathizers, and the repression of political groups with communist tendencies (Cumings 2005). At a point in time when many Koreans may have harboured sympathies towards a movement that promised that all people would be equal, the United States and conservative forces made sure that it did not take hold in the southern half.

Furthermore, the United States would of course be a key reason why North Korea was unable to defeat the South during the Korean War. USAMGIK dissolved in August 1948, on the day that South Korea was proclaimed. Over the next few months, US troops would leave the country. The last of them departed the Korean Peninsula in early 1950 (Stueck 1997). Around the same time, the US government left South Korea outside of its security perimeter in East Asia and the US Congress rejected a South Korean aid package. In other words, Washington essentially indicated that the security of South Korea was none of its business, unlike Japan or the Philippines, which were included in the perimeter (Stueck 1997). Arguably, this helped encourage Kim Il-sung to take the decision to launch an invasion of the South in June.

The United States, of course, quickly mobilized its political leverage to ensure that the UN Security Council authorized the use of force to repel North Korea's invasion.[1] This allowed the United States to put

1 The Soviet Union was boycotting the UN Security Council at the time, in protest at China not being granted a seat on the Council in favour of Taiwan. Therefore,

together a UN force also comprising 15 other countries. Yet it was mainly a US force, with Washington deploying around 1.78 million soldiers during the war – far more than any other country bar the two Koreas themselves and China (Cha & Pacheco Pardo 2023). Without the support of US troops, it would have been very difficult for South Korea to push back against the invading forces from the North. Which is why, even today, most South Koreans are grateful to the United States and large majorities support their country's alliance with Washington.

The flip side of the coin is that arguably North Korea was not able to reunify the Korean Peninsula by force and on its own terms because of the intervention of the United States. What is more, the combined UN/US–South Korean forces were able to push the Korean People's Army all the way to the Amrok River by the autumn of 1950. It seemed as if South Korea was about to take control of the whole of the Korean Peninsula and reunify Korea under its rule. This is when Chinese leader Mao Zedong decided to deploy the People's Volunteer Army in support of North Korea. The intervention of these Chinese troops helped to draw the Korean War into a stalemate around the 38th parallel. Arguably, this further enraged North Korea. Over the decades, the Kim family has ensured that North Korea's official propaganda emphasizes that the Korean War was fought between North Korea and the United States, in support of its "puppet" South Korea, while de-emphasizing the role of China in the confrontation (Seth 2018).

Furthermore, the US Air Force carpet-bombed North Korea throughout the war. The United States dropped a total of 635,000 tons of bombs: communication infrastructure and industrial facilities that could be used in support of the war effort were targeted first; cities and towns followed, including civilian facilities such as schools or town halls. By the end of the war, 75 per cent of Pyongyang laid in ruins and key centres such as Hamhung, Nampo and Wonsan were even more heavily destroyed. North Korea essentially laid in ruins, with hundreds of thousands of North Koreans killed by B-29s and other US aircraft engaged in the bombing campaign (Cumings 2010). The US Air Force had dropped

---

Moscow was not able to exercise its veto power to prevent the vote in support of South Korea. Shortly afterwards, the Soviet Union returned to its seat at the Council after realizing the mistake that the boycott had been.

more bombs in North Korea than it had in the whole of the Pacific theatre during the Second World War (Cumings 2010).

Washington's bombing campaign was a key driver informing Pyongyang's hatred towards its "enemy" in the early stages of the relationship between the two. To this day, North Korea's school textbooks, museums and other propaganda materials continue to emphasize the extent to which the North Korean population and the country's cities and infrastructure suffered as a result of US bombs (Seth 2018). The Kim family has made sure to remind new generations of North Koreans about it, as a way to try to rally the population around its leadership but also to portray its military-focused policy as a means to prevent this from happening again. But it should be acknowledged that the bombing campaign was a reason why North Korea identified itself in opposition to the United States, at least in its formative years, as much as Washington's overall role in preventing Pyongyang from defeating Seoul during the Korean War.

Shortly after the Korean War, the United States concluded an official alliance with South Korea. On 1 October 1953, as the ink on the armistice agreement putting an end to the Korean War had barely dried, Seoul and Washington signed "the relationship forged in blood". This was a reference to the 990,000 South Korean soldiers and 36,000 American servicemen killed during the war (Heo & Roehrig 2018). Seven decades later, the South Korea–US alliance remains a cornerstone in South Korea's defence strategy and a key component of Washington's military strategy in East Asia and beyond. De jure, the alliance is entrusted with defending South Korea against a potential North Korean invasion. Consequently, the United States has a formal role in the event of a new military confrontation on the Korean Peninsula. And it should be remembered that technically the Korean War is yet to end, since the 1953 armistice put an end to hostilities but is not a peace agreement. In other words, technically the United States and North Korea remain at war while the former is committed to the protection of South Korea.

From a North Korean perspective, the enduring South Korea–US alliance is a key reason why Pyongyang has been unable to attempt a new invasion of South Korea, particularly throughout the 1950s and 1960s, when the North could credibly argue that it had a stronger army and economy than the South. In fact, in the 1970s Kim discussed the possibility of launching a strike on South Korea with Mao. This conversation occurred in the context of Washington's decision to "abandon" South Vietnam to end the Vietnam War, and as the Richard Nixon administration was seeking diplomatic normalization with China while simultaneously reducing the number of US troops in South Korea. From Pyongyang's perspective, this could have led to the belief that the United States would simply remove its troops from South Korea on the advent of a second Korean War. However, Mao advised Kim against such a move, and the United States reiterated its commitment to the alliance with South Korea (Heo & Roehrig 2018). In other words, the South Korea–US alliance has even survived periods in which the United States has withdrawn its support to other partners and allies, therefore putting a break to North Korea's potential aspirations to take the South by force.

Moving back to the role of ideology in informing decades of North Korean hostility towards the United States, the role of USAMGIK in preventing communism from taking hold in the southern half of Korea in the aftermath of Korea's independence continued during the authoritarian South Korean regimes of Rhee Syngman, Park Chung-hee and Chun Doo-hwan. But these three leaders had the support of successive US presidents, who came to see South Korea as a stalwart against the spread of communism across East Asia. According to the Domino Theory prevalent during the Cold War, the fall of one government to communism would lead to the spread of communism to neighbouring states (Ninkovich 1994). In this respect, South Korea was as important as West Germany in preventing the spread of communism, even if the experience of Vietnam demonstrated that the theory did not hold. Yet Washington's efforts to support Seoul necessarily created an ideological confrontation with Pyongyang.

Throughout the Cold War, therefore, North Korea was one of the many countries in the communist camp hostile to the United States because of what Washington represented in economic and socio-political terms: capitalism and democracy. North Korea's focus on communist principles as a crucial guide for its way of life was therefore anathema to the values that the United States embodied and that Washington sought to spread across East Asia and beyond. Even if North Korea played China and the Soviet Union against each other for its own economic and political benefit, Kim remained committed to the communist camp. As a case in point, his international trips throughout his time in office were almost all to countries with impeccable communist credentials (Suh 1995).

Eventually, North Korea would also join the Non-Aligned Movement. Pyongyang formally became part of the group in August 1975. And while it did not renege on its formal alliances with China and the Soviet Union nor did it move away from its links with the communist camp, membership of the Non-Aligned Movement created a new point of ideological friction with the United States.[2] The movement advocated – and continues to advocate – policies such as the rejection of imperialism and colonialism, non-aggression and respect for territorial sovereignty, and cooperation and solidarity among its members (Arnold 2006). From a North Korean perspective, the United States was and is guilty of all of these. Thus membership of the Non-Aligned Movement was yet another ideological rebuke to the values that Pyongyang thinks Washington represents.

Throughout the Cold War, North Korea's hostility towards the United States sometimes heated up. In January 1968, North Korea seized the spy ship USS *Pueblo*. According to Pyongyang, the *Pueblo* had entered North Korea's territorial waters, a point denied by Washington, which maintained that the ship was in international waters. After 11 months in captivity, the 82 surviving crew members were released in December 1968 (Mobley 2003). Yet shortly after, in April 1969, North Korea shot down an EC-121, killing its 31 crew members. This was a US reconnaissance plane involved in routine data collection operations in and around the Korean Peninsula. Two North Korean MiG-21s were involved in the shooting, with Pyongyang making the allegation that it had entered the country's air space and the United States rejecting this accusation (Mobley 2003). Seven years later, in August 1976, North Korean soldiers killed two US army officers who were trimming a tree in the Joint Security Area located inside the DMZ. The North Korean government argued that the murdered soldiers had attacked North Korean

2 Incidentally and ironically when considering North Korea's membership, the Non-Aligned Movement can trace its origins to the aftermath of the Korean War and the decision by many countries to side neither with the US-led bloc nor the Soviet Union- and China-led bloc.

servicemen (New York Times 1976). On top of these more serious cases, there were multiple instances of shooting exchanges across the DMZ. In short, the Cold War that pitched the US-led capitalist bloc against the Soviet-led communist bloc sometimes became a direct conflict between the United States and North Korea across the DMZ.

Following the end of the Cold War, North Korea's enmity towards the United States has continued on the grounds of ideological differences and Washington's commitment to the South Korea–US alliance. Even as the Kim family has moved away from communist principles, its dictatorial rule and anti-capitalist economy creates an obvious ideological divergence with Washington. In this sense, North Korea can find points of ideological discrepancy with the United States because, simply put, their systems differ. On top of that, North Korea has been one of the staunchest critics of US interventionism in foreign affairs, particularly the invasions of Afghanistan and Iraq during the George W. Bush presidency (Pacheco Pardo 2019). More recently, North Korea has been one of the very few countries to side decisively with Russia in criticizing NATO's "expansionism" as a reason for Vladimir Putin's decision to invade Ukraine (Pacheco Pardo & Kim 2023b). In Pyongyang's eyes, the United States continues to be an imperialist power leading other countries to contain North Korea itself as well as other countries challenging Washington's policies.

As for the South Korea–US alliance, it continues to be on solid footing as over 90 per cent of South Koreans and a substantial majority of Americans routinely express their support for it (Woo 2016). The South Korea of 2024 has stronger conventional military capabilities than the North (International Institute for Strategic Studies 2023). Yet this does not mean that South Korean leaders or the general population question the value of the alliance. If anything, the alliance has become more globally oriented, which only reinforces its value to the two partners. North Korea's unsuccessful attempts to drive a wedge between the two allies over the decades have only served to reinforce the commitment of Seoul and Washington to their bilateral relationship.

Since the end of the Cold War, there has been a new point of friction between Pyongyang and Washington: North Korea's economic development. Since North Korea has no diplomatic relations with the United States and is subject to American and international sanctions, the vast majority of international investors have shunned North Korea as an investment destination. Furthermore, Pyongyang is unable to join the World Bank and the International Monetary Fund (IMF) as a result of its poor relationship with the United States (Nicolai da Costa 2018). As a result, North Korea has become increasingly critical of what it deems to be a form of economic warfare on the part of the United States. Washington, meanwhile, maintains that the door for economic cooperation with Pyongyang is open as long as the Kim family relinquishes its nuclear weapons.

Having first started to hold conversations with North Korean officials in the late 2000s, I can attest that the United States is perceived as a hostile force bent on ending North Korea. That is, the United States is regarded as a country obsessed with ending the Kim regime. North Korean officials are undeniably critical of what they see as US imperialism, whether in East Asia, the Middle East or elsewhere. They also argue that the United States should respect the North Korean system and way of thinking, in the same way that, they maintain, North Korea does not seek to change the United States' way of life. Certainly, there is no love lost between the North Korean officials that I get to meet and the United States. At some point, it is necessary to recognize that this is probably not a façade but rather deeply rooted mistrust.

Yet it should also be noted that in private North Korean officials also indicate their willingness to talk to the United States and find ways to improve the relationship. And they also express that North Korea does not have the type of historical problems with the United States that it has with, for example, Japan (the former colonial power). Certainly, these could simply be talking points intended to confuse the interlocutor, but having listened to multiple North Koreans speak in these terms for over a decade, we should also be open to the possibility of considering that North Korea would like to have a different type of relationship with the United States. As of 2024, in any case, North Korea's official rhetoric continues to emphasize that Pyongyang considers Washington to be an enemy and hostile country, which seeks to remove the Kim regime from power, by force if necessary. Thus, hostility towards the United States remains a foundational and fundamental characteristic for North Korea.

SEEKING RECOGNITION AS A "NORMAL" COUNTRY: THE UNITED STATES AND BEYOND

China in the 1970s under Mao Zedong. Iraq in the 1980s under Saddam Hussein. Vietnam in the 1990s under its Communist Party. Libya in the 2000s under Muammar Gaddafi. Cuba in the 2010s under Raul Castro. The list of countries, leaders and families that in theory had the United States as "enemy number one" but then in practice launched diplomatic normalization processes with Washington is long. These five cases spanning five decades are good examples of the lure of diplomatic relations with the United States, regardless of who is in the White House. A leader who can (re-)establish diplomatic relations with the American superpower can gain domestic and international prestige and dream about the economic, diplomatic and sometimes even security benefits that this will bring.

The Kim family is no exception to this situation. Kim Il-sung, Kim Jong-il and Kim Jong-un have all sought to meet the "leader of the free world", to facilitate North Korea and the United States establishing diplomatic relations. Three generations of the Kim family have understood that the potential benefits of having a formal relationship with the United States probably outweigh any drawbacks. After all, the key idea underpinning *Juche* is that North Korea should have independence of action. This includes the autonomy for North Korea to forge its own foreign relations. And the Kims may be exceptional in the way in which they have been able to create the only hereditary communist regime in history. But they are normal in that they see diplomatic relations with the United States as a key goal, in common to multiple leaders of authoritarian and dictatorial regimes throughout history and across different parts of the world. So long as the United States continues to be the biggest and most dynamic economy in the world as well as a diplomatic and military superpower, its appeal will endure.

North Korea's first real attempt to set its relationship with the United States in a more positive direction took place in the 1970s. On 25 March 1974, North Korea's rubber-stamp Supreme People's Assembly wrote an official letter to the US Congress requesting that the two countries establish bilateral diplomatic relations.[3] The United States declined this request, but Pyongyang remained undeterred. In September 1978, Kim Il-sung proposed the establishment of official bilateral relations with the United States during a speech to commemorate the 30th anniversary of the founding of North Korea (Korea and World Affairs 1985). Kim's proposal came as the United States and China were about to finalize their own diplomatic normalization process, concluded on 1 January 1979. Once again, Pyongyang's proposal did not gain traction in Washington. Simply put, US leaders had no interest in launching a diplomatic normalization process with North Korea, not least because of opposition from South Korean leaders. From their perspective, North Korea was trying to drive a wedge in the South Korea–US alliance and use normalization with the United States as a means to have US troops leave South Korea (Pacheco Pardo 2019). To North Korea's chagrin, the United States would always prioritize its relationship with South Korea over potential normalization with the North.

Having said that, Kim had good reasons to believe that the United States may have been more receptive to his suggestion of normalization. The 1970s was a time of geopolitical change for the United States in Asia. To begin with and most memorably, US President Richard Nixon, a Republican, shocked the world when he visited China in February 1972 and met with Mao Zedong. Nixon was certainly aware of the Sino–Soviet split that neither side could continue to hide. And he thought that he could bring China closer to the United States with his political gamble, thus undermining the position of the Soviet Union both globally and within the communist camp (Nixon 1978). Theirs was a gamble that paid off. Subsequent US and Chinese leaders continued to push for normalization. US President Jimmy Carter, a Democrat, and Deng Xiaoping, in the midst of launching a process of economic opening up, took the final step in establishing Sino–American diplomatic relations in 1979. From a North Korean perspective, this could easily be interpreted as US leaders being comfortable in dealing with a communist regime if it suited their goals. Indeed, there was the added political twist

3 The Supreme People's Assembly of the Democratic People's Republic of Korea. "The Letter to the Congress of the United States of America". 25 March 1974.

that the United States switched diplomatic recognition from Taiwan to China, therefore weakening its ties with an ally out of self-interest.

At the same time, the Nixon administration also launched a process to disentangle the United States from the Vietnam War. In January 1973, the United States, North Vietnam and South Vietnam signed the Paris Peace Accords to end the war. This was basically a way for Washington to save face, since domestic opposition to the war in the United States had made it politically impossible to continue the fight against North Vietnam. Within two years, all American troops had left Vietnam and the North had taken over the South, thereby establishing communist rule over the whole of reunified Vietnam (Nixon 1978). The United States seemingly found it acceptable to effectively hand over one of its allies, South Vietnam, to a communist foe, the stronger North Vietnam, to cut its losses, a decision not too dissimilar to Washington's shifting policy towards China and Taiwan. This move would have only further encouraged North Korea to think that the United States may consider diplomatic normalization even at the expense of its relationship with South Korea, if it suited US interests.

Notwithstanding the international context and even a period of improving inter-Korean relations during the time of the 1972 joint communiqué between South and North (see Chapter 4), North Korea would be unable to follow in the footsteps of China in terms of its relationship with the United States. Yet a new opportunity for the Kim regime to improve relations with Washington would present itself in the late 1980s. In 1987, US President Ronald Reagan agreed to American diplomats interacting with North Korean counterparts during social occasions. One year later, Reagan allowed unofficial exchanges and diplomatic contacts as well. On taking office, former US Vice President and newly sworn-in President George H. W. Bush continued the same policy. Therefore, Washington and Pyongyang had their most senior meeting ever in 1992: US Undersecretary of State for Political Affairs Arnold Kanter and Workers' Party of Korea Secretary for International Affairs Kim Young-sun held a meeting at the US Mission to the United Nations (UN) (Reuters 1992). The first contacts between the two sides prompted Kim to give a rare interview to the *Washington Times* in 1992, in which he called for diplomatic normalization between his country and the United States (Shiner 1992).

Once again, the international context had provided North Korea with an opportunity to seek diplomatic relations with the United States. Throughout the latter half of the 1980s, Reagan and his new Soviet counterpart, Mikhail Gorbachev, launched a process of détente to improve relations between Washington and Moscow. Afterwards, the collapse of the Soviet Union in 1991 had put an end to the Cold War while China continued its process of opening up, which was briefly interrupted following the crackdown on the Tiananmen Square protests of 1989 (Kramer 1990). In the meantime, South Korea had transitioned from dictatorship to democracy in 1987–8. The new South Korean president, Roh Tae-woo, had launched his *Nordpolitik*, borrowing the name from West Germany's *Ostpolitik*, to improve inter-Korean relations but also calling for the United States and Japan to establish links with North Korea (see Chapter 4 for more details) (Roh 1988). These processes had also opened the door for the two Koreas to join the UN, which they both did simultaneously in September 1991 (UN 2023a).

Yet North Korea once again failed to establish diplomatic relations with the United States. Furthermore, South Korea normalized relations with the Soviet Union in 1990 and with China in 1992. The fact that North Korea's two treaty allies had agreed to normalization with Seoul even if the United Stated did not reciprocate with Pyongyang was a major blow to Kim. From Washington's perspective, normalization was not a priority since it was assumed that North Korea would collapse, as communist regimes across central and eastern Europe were doing one after another at the time (Kim 2006a). In essence, Beijing and Moscow saw relations with Seoul as part of their future. Whereas, in sharp contrast, Washington saw no future in a possible relationship with Pyongyang.

North Korea has continued to seek diplomatic normalization with the United States since the end of the Cold War. Kim Il-sung died in July 1994. Thus, it was up to Kim Jong-il to continue his father's quest for normalization. On his taking office, Pyongyang was in the middle of the first North Korean nuclear crisis, having announced its intention to withdraw from the Nuclear Non-Proliferation Treaty (NPT) in January 1993 (Horvitz 1993). Pyongyang did not initially carry out its threat. Instead, there was a negotiation process with Washington to put an end to the crisis. With negotiations between the two countries stalled, former President Jimmy Carter became the first former US leader to visit North Korea and met with Kim Il-sung only a few weeks before the North Korean leader passed away. This paved the way for the United States, under Bill Clinton's leadership, and North Korea to sign the Agreed Framework between the United States of America and the Democratic People's Republic of Korea in October 1994. The agreement was essentially a bargain whereby Pyongyang agreed to freeze and reverse its nuclear programme in exchange for Washington providing economic support and agreeing to normalize diplomatic relations. As per article 2 of the Agreed Framework, "the two sides [would] move toward full normalization of political and economic relations".[4] From a North Korean perspective, this was the holy grail that it had sought for decades. The Agreed Framework would serve as the template for three similar agreements that North Korea would reach with the George W. Bush, Barack Obama and Donald Trump administrations.

With North Korea suffering from the Arduous March throughout the mid-1990s and the Republican-controlled US Congress curtailing implementation of the Agreed Framework, Pyongyang was unable to make progress in its relationship with Washington. Yet the United States provided aid to North Korea via the World Food Programme during these years. This gesture indicated that the United States was not necessarily opposed to providing humanitarian aid to North Korea and perhaps even broader economic support. The political environment further changed in the late 1990s, after Kim Dae-jung took office in South Korea and launched his "Sunshine Policy". The Clinton administration used this as an opportunity to try to improve relations with North Korea. Thus, First Vice Chairman of the National Defense Commission Jo Myong-rok became the highest-ranked North Korean official ever to set foot in the White House when he met with Clinton in October 2000. Formally, Jo was second in the North Korean hierarchy, only below Kim Jong-il himself. One week later, US Secretary of State Madeleine Albright travelled to Pyongyang and famously toasted with Kim himself (Koh 2000). Clinton contemplated the possibility of holding a summit

4 Agreed Framework between the United States of America and the Democratic People's Republic of Korea. Geneva. 21 October 1994.

with Kim, but his presidency was coming to an end and the meeting did not take place (Clinton 2004).

From a North Korean perspective, the Clinton years served to imprint the idea that the United Stated would pay attention to their country if there was a nuclear threat, as had been the case during the first nuclear crisis. They also affirmed that the United States was receptive to considering better relations with North Korea when its allies and partners were doing the same. So even though the Kim regime had failed to normalize relations with the United States, it seemed to understand the way to achieve its decades-old goal. Pyongyang would thus test these two ideas during the Bush years.

George W. Bush came to office with an "Anything But Clinton" policy, which included criticism of the Agreed Framework on the grounds that Washington was offering too much to Pyongyang in return for too little. Bush even included North Korea in his (in)famous "Axis of Evil", a term he first used in his January 2002 State of the Union Address (The White House 2002), which came only five months after the 9/11 terrorist attacks on US soil. Along with Iran and Iraq, North Korea was the only other member of this axis as initially presented by Bush. This clearly indicated that the improvement in relations towards the end of the Clinton administration was at an end.

Yet the Kim government was busy laying the groundwork to create the conditions to improve relations with the United States. In 2000–1, Pyongyang established diplomatic relations with the EU, Canada, Italy, Germany, Spain, the UK and a host of other Western countries. There was a clear message for Washington: North Korea was open to diplomatic relations with the West. Even more importantly, Japanese Prime Minister Koizumi Junichiro travelled to Pyongyang in September 2002 to meet with Kim. This way, he became Japan's first – and so far the last – leader to meet his North Korean counterpart. Tokyo and Pyongyang issued the Japan–DPRK Pyongyang Declaration, calling for "an early normalisation of the [diplomatic] relations" between the two countries.[5] In other words, Washington's closest ally in Asia was also considering diplomatic relations with North Korea. And in the meantime, Kim Dae-jung continued to press ahead with his Sunshine Policy. For the

5 Japan–DPRK Pyongyang Declaration. Pyongyang. 17 September 2002.

Kim family, this could only mean that diplomatic normalization with the United States should be within reach considering that its friends and allies were seeking better relations with Pyongyang.

North Korea's plans, however, once again failed to bear fruit. In October 2002, the Bush administration sent a delegation to North Korea. The delegation confronted North Korean officials with evidence that their government was pursuing a clandestine enriched uranium-based nuclear programme, in violation of the terms of the Agreed Framework. First Vice Foreign Minister Kang Suk-ju admitted to the programme. Within weeks, the Bush administration had effectively finalized the Agreed Framework. In January 2003, Pyongyang once again threatened withdrawal from the NPT. This time, it carried through with its threat. In April, North Korea became the first and, as of 2024, the only country in history to leave the agreement (IAEA 2023). In the meantime, normalization talks between Japan and North Korea collapsed, as Pyongyang failed to provide a satisfactory answer to Tokyo's demands about the whereabouts of several Japanese citizens who had been abducted in the past (Funabashi 2007). North Korea's strategy was thus in tatters.

Pyongyang's withdrawal from the NPT precipitated the second North Korean nuclear crisis. This time, the United States and North Korea engaged in the Six-Party Talks, a process that also involved South Korea, China, Japan and Russia. From the perspective of the Bush administration, bilateral talks leading to the Agreed Framework had been counterproductive. Instead, the United States wished to bring China into the resolution of the North Korean nuclear issue. It was also necessary to have South Korea involved in the process, which had not been the case during the Agreed Framework discussions (Funabashi 2007). The outcome, in any case, was very similar to that of the Agreed Framework. In September 2005, the six parties issued the Joint Statement of the Fourth Round of the Six-Party Talks. The joint statement essentially reiterated the principle that Washington would offer Pyongyang diplomatic normalization and economic relations in exchange for denuclearization.[6] In a sense the Bush administration had arrived at exactly the point where the Clinton administration had been over a decade earlier.

6 Joint Statement of the Fourth Round of the Six-Party Talks. Beijing. 19 September 2005.

North Korea's first-ever nuclear test in October 2006, however, once again had a negative effect on the prospect of US–North Korea diplomatic normalization. The Bush administration responded to the test by rallying the UN Security Council, including China and Russia, to impose sanctions on North Korea. From then on, a mixture of UN and autonomous sanctions became Washington's main approach towards Pyongyang. Indeed, the Six-Party Talks collapsed in 2008. Kim's health problems also stalled decision-making processes in North Korea, which were more focused on domestic succession politics than its relations with the outside world (Cha & Pacheco Pardo 2023). The Obama administration came to office in 2009 and ended up launching a policy of "strategic patience" to deal with North Korea. Essentially, this meant ignoring Pyongyang and focusing on other foreign policy issues that were more pressing from Washington's perspective. Former presidents Clinton and Carter visited North Korea, the former in 2009 and the latter in 2010 and 2011, but to no avail (Pacheco Pardo 2019). After Kim Jong-un replaced his father in December 2011, there was a brief period of negotiations. This resulted in the "Leap Day" deal, signed in February 2012 and which once again reiterated the principle of North Korean denuclearization in exchange for normalization with the United States (Nuland 2012). The deal, however, was not implemented after North Korea conducted a rocket test in violation of UN sanctions related to its nuclear programme. At the third time of asking, neither North Korea, especially, nor the United States were ready to implement their side of the bargain.

North Korea and the United States did not resume potential normalization talks until 2018. Once again, the political environment provided the conditions for talks to take place. In South Korea, the liberal Moon Jae-in took office in May 2017 after two consecutive conservative presidents. Moon sought rapprochement with North Korea and made use of the PyeongChang Winter Olympic Games of February 2018 to launch an inter-Korean dialogue process (see Chapter 4). In the case of the United States, Trump took office with a strong belief in his own ability to use personal diplomacy to change the policy of other countries. As explained in the opening vignette of this chapter, this included North Korea, leading to the Singapore Summit of June 2018. A second summit followed in February 2019, plus a third meeting in the DMZ, also including Moon, in June of the same year. During this meeting, Trump briefly stepped into the North Korean side of the DMZ. This way, he became the first sitting US president to "visit" North Korea (Lee 2019).

The potential normalization process, however, did not move ahead as Trump's erratic foreign policy and Kim's hesitance at taking decisive steps towards denuclearization stalled any potential progress. At the time, I had the chance to meet North Korean officials on several occasions. There was a clear desire on the part of North Korea to advance relations with the United States, both to improve the economic situation of their country and to use normalization with Washington as a springboard to expand relations with other countries as well. But at the same time, North Korean interlocutors made it clear that their country's nuclear programme, from their perspective, was a necessary deterrent for the Kim family to avoid the fate of the Taliban in Afghanistan, Hussein in Iraq or Gaddafi in Libya. The three of them had been removed from power by or with the support of the United States, according to the North Korean narrative. In a particularly testy exchange in late 2017 somewhere in Europe, a period in which Trump and Kim were trading insults and threats, a North Korean official shouted "never" when they were asked under what conditions North Korea would be willing to give up its nuclear weapons. While unsurprising, the intensity of the response was very telling.

Herein lies North Korea's dilemma when it comes to diplomatic normalization with the United States. Pyongyang does not want to give up its nuclear programme. This should be self-evident decades after Pyongyang started development of the programme and more than 15 years after its first nuclear test (see Chapter 5 for further details). But the United States insists that bilateral diplomatic normalization goes hand in hand with North Korean denuclearization, a policy that US President Joe Biden maintains. Pyongyang and Washington are thus at odds, in a seemingly unsolvable quagmire.

FIGHTING "THE EMPIRE": NORTH KOREA AND ITS "ALLIES" AND PARTNERS

It is often said that North Korea is the most isolated country on earth, given its *Juche* ideology, limited diplomacy, secluded economy and disengagement from most international institutions. But this assertion is misleading. North Korea does have allies and diplomatic partners. In particular, North Korea has long been close to countries that share an enmity towards the United States or that at least have a problematic relationship with it. In other words, North Korea has long been close with countries with which the United States has problematic relations. This dates back to the very foundation of North Korea in 1948, was reinforced during the Korean War and the Cold War, and continues to be the case today. The latest example is North Korea's support for Russia's war of aggression against US- and NATO-supported Ukraine.

Arguably, China is North Korea's strongest and longest-standing partner, with the relationship between both tracing its roots to the years leading to the foundation of the People's Republic in 1949. China and Korea had a centuries-old relationship, with Korea serving as a tributary state to China and being influenced by its neighbour, yet also seeking to preserve its unique culture and political independence. Towards the end of the nineteenth century, Korea broke ranks with China as it sought to launch its own modernization path. Yet Japanese colonialism brought Korea and China closer to each other again. Korean independence units fought alongside Chinese guerrillas to liberate Korea, Manchuria and other territories occupied by Japan throughout the 1930s and 1940s (Cumings 2005). And once Korea was liberated, Korean communist troops continued to fight along with their Chinese counterparts still involved in the Chinese Civil War against the Kuomintang (Cumings 2005). This created strong bonds between the future leaders and peoples of China and North Korea. Unsurprisingly, China then established diplomatic relations with North Korea in October 1949, barely five days after its establishment.

China and North Korea forged even closer relations during the Korean War. Mao acquiesced to Kim's plans to invade South Korea in the months before the start of the war. More importantly, Chinese troops were essential in preserving the very existence of North Korea when Mao sent them across the Amrok River as South Korea and US-led UN troops were about to reach the Sino–North Korean border. In October 1950, the People's Volunteer Army (PVA) thus joined the war. The PVA was composed of members of the People's Liberation Army, who were nominally volunteers to prevent China from formally being at war with the United States. Up to three million Chinese troops and civilians served during the war (Stueck 1997). Among them was Mao Anying, Mao's eldest son, who was killed during an air raid the month after Chinese troops first set foot on the Korean Peninsula. In total, more than 180,000 Chinese soldiers died during the war (Stueck 1997).

Russia arguably is North Korea's second strongest partner. Soviet and Korean troops fought side by side during the Second World War, as they sought to expel Japan from the Korean Peninsula and Manchuria. Soviet forces were then the first foreign contingent to arrive in the Korean Peninsula in 1945, occupying the territory above the 38th parallel and thus guaranteeing that Kim Il-sung, Moscow's preferred candidate, would become the ruler of North Korea. The Soviet Union was then the first country to formally recognize North Korea upon its establishment. And in March 1949, Kim made his first foreign trip as leader of North Korea to the Soviet Union to meet with Stalin.

In early 1950, the Soviet Union also acquiesced to Kim's decision to launch an invasion of South Korea. Officially, the Soviet Union did not participate in the war. Once the United States had ensured that the Soviet-less UN Security Council allowed the dispatch of UN forces in support of South Korea, the Soviet Union wanted to avoid a direct confrontation between its troops and those of the United States. Therefore, Stalin refused to send troops or military vehicles to the Korean Peninsula. However, Soviet MiG-15s were dispatched and Soviet pilots went into combat against US counterparts. Furthermore, Soviet generals supported North Korea's strategic planning and the Soviet Union provided logistical support as well as medicines (Stueck 1997). In short, Soviet support was essential for North Korea during the Korean War.

North Korea, China and the Soviet Union all had an interest in confronting the United States for ideological reasons. Following the war, China and the Soviet Union both offered materials and experts for North Korea to rebuild its cities, infrastructure and industry. Meanwhile, Kim visited the Soviet Union and China immediately after the war to thank his benefactors (Cha 2018). Yet Stalin had passed away and Khrushchev was busy denouncing his predecessor and Stalinism more generally while also seeking better relations with the United States. This led to a growing ideological split between Khrushchev and Mao. By the 1950s,

China and the Soviet Union were involved in an ideological battle. In 1961, the Sino–Soviet split was made official as Beijing and Moscow fought for the leadership of the communist camp (Shen 2020).

Aware of these divisions, North Korea and other communist countries sought to exploit the gap between the Soviet Union and China for their own gain. In the case of Pyongyang, it signed a Treaty of Friendship, Co-operation and Mutual Assistance with the Soviet Union on 6 July 1961 and another treaty with exactly the same title with China five days later. Moscow and Beijing were now treaty allies with Pyongyang. Throughout the Cold War, North Korea would seek to extract benefits from its relationship with both countries by playing one off against the other. In general, Kim maintained cordial relations with both countries. Sometimes those relations soured. Most notably, Kim was shocked when Mao launched a rapprochement process with the United States in the early 1970s (Shen 2020). But more generally, North Korea relied on both China and the Soviet Union to ensure that it had their backing in its ideological confrontation with South Korea and the United States. In spite of a nominal *Juche* policy, Kim understood very well the benefits of having close relations with the two strongest countries in the communist camp, both of which happened to share a border with North Korea.

Anther key source of support for North Korea during these decades came from fellow communist countries. Mongolia and North Vietnam were two of the first countries to recognize North Korea, and they provided material and political support to Pyongyang during the Korean War. In 1956, Kim would pay a visit to Mongolia and two years later, in 1958, he would go to North Vietnam. North Korea would then go on to send troops and pilots in support of North Vietnam during the Vietnam War (Pribbenow 2011). Likewise, central and eastern European countries in the communist camp rapidly established diplomatic relations with North Korea throughout 1948–9. Six of them would go on to also provide material and diplomatic support to North Korea during the Korean War: Bulgaria, Czechoslovakia, East Germany, Hungary, Poland and Romania. Five thousand North Korean orphans were also sent to central and eastern European countries during and in the immediate aftermath of the war (Pacheco Pardo 2021a).

After the war, central and eastern European countries also sent materials and experts to North Korea to help rebuild and upgrade sectors such as agriculture, health care and industry. In 1956, Kim embarked on a tour of the Soviet Union and seven countries across central and eastern Europe. Throughout the rest of the Cold War, Kim would continue to work together with European countries in the communist bloc and visit the region on occasion. In the other direction, East Germany's Eric Honecker, Romania's Nicolae Ceausescu and Yugoslavia's Josip Broz "Tito" were among the communist leaders who visited North Korea. In particular, Kim would establish a good rapport with Ceausescu, the president of Romania, with whom he shared a strong personality cult (Pacheco Pardo 2021a). These countries were in the Soviet orbit and firmly in the communist camp, hence their good relationship with North Korea since nominally all of them were opposed to "American imperialism". At the same time, they were smaller powers within this camp, a characteristic that they shared with North Korea and that helps explain the affinity that Kim felt with them. Cooperation with other smaller communist countries was at least partially a means to try to check on Soviet and Chinese influence over the communist camp.

Membership of the Non-Aligned Movement also gave North Korea a platform to confront the United States without the support of China and the Soviet Union. Unable to join the UN because of the division of Korea, Pyongyang became an active participant in the activities of the movement after officially becoming a member in 1975. However, North Korea was unable to use membership of this organization to push for the isolation of South Korea (Pak 2000). This was one of the key reasons why Pyongyang had joined and showed the limits of North Korean diplomacy to advance the foreign policy goals of the country.

Arguably more successful during the Cold War period was the Korean People's Army's role in supporting anti-imperialist and anti-colonial movements fighting against the United States, US-backed forces or their (Western) colonial powers. North Korea was actively involved in providing material and technical support to these movements, which was particularly valuable since North Korean troops had experience fighting against Japanese colonial forces and, during the Korean War, against US forces (Young 2021a). Yet once again North Korea was unable to make skilful use of diplomacy to ensure that its (welcome) material and technical support could lead to the isolation of South Korea or to broader goals related to North Korea's confrontation with the United States.

This became a purely transactional relationship showing the limits of ideological affinity in supporting North Korea's goals.

In fact, towards the end of the Cold War it became clear that Sino–American rapprochement and South Korea's own growing economic power trumped North Korea's ideological affinity with fellow communist countries and (post)colonial states. This was vividly illustrated by the Seoul Olympic Games of 1988. The Kim regime launched a full-blown diplomatic campaign to ensure that the communist bloc boycotted the games. It should be remembered that the American bloc had boycotted Moscow 1980, led by the United States itself, and the communist bloc had reciprocated with a boycott of Los Angeles 1984, led by the Soviet Union in this case. Therefore, Kim Il-sung could be confident that the communist bloc would attend to its request to boycott the games held by Washington's "puppet". In the end, and North Korea aside, Cuba was the only country to formally boycott the games, and even this seemed to be related to Havana's anger at having failed in its bid to host the 1987 Pan-American Games. This was a huge diplomatic blow for Kim, demonstrating the limits of the supposed communist brotherhood in leading to support for a core North Korean objective.

The situation became even worse for North Korea in the late 1980s and early 1990s. One communist country after another decided to establish diplomatic relations with South Korea, including China and Vietnam in 1992 and 1995, respectively. The Soviet Union dissolved, and Russia and the newly independent countries that had been controlled from Moscow improved relations with the United States. China and Russia then decided to end their support for the North Korean economy, thus exacerbating the effects of the famine that took over the country in the mid-1990s (Cha 2018). It seemed that Pyongyang's former partners and allies, as much as the United States, were expecting North Korea to collapse and be absorbed by the South. After all, this had been the fate of an East Germany now integrated by West Germany.

Yet North Korea proved resilient. By the late 1990s and early 2000s, Kim Jong-il was ready to continue to deal with the United States with the support of China and Russia. Crucially for Kim, a new president took office in Russia in 2000 who wanted to restore the greatness that he thought his country had lost following the collapse of the Soviet Union: Vladimir Putin. In February 2000, Moscow and Pyongyang signed a new

Treaty of Friendship, Good Neighbourliness and Cooperation to replace to defunct Soviet-era agreement. And in July, Putin travelled to North Korea to meet with Kim. The North Korean leader would reciprocate the visit in 2001 and 2002. Equally relevant, Russia resumed large-scale economic and energy assistance to North Korea and became a strong diplomatic partner (Takeda 2006). Both were crucial for Pyongyang, particularly in the context of deteriorating relations between North Korea and the United States after George W. Bush had taken office in Washington.

Meanwhile, relations between North Korea and China also improved. Kim visited China in 2000 and 2001 to meet with Jiang Zemin. The Chinese leader also travelled to North Korea in April 2001, his first trip to China's neighbour in 11 years. Hu Jintao then visited North Korea in 2005 after taking over from Jiang. Kim, meanwhile, visited Hu in 2004 and 2006. It could be said that Putin had kick-started a new round of competition between Beijing and Moscow to influence Pyongyang. And China rose to become North Korea's main trade and investment partner, eventually becoming the Kim regime's economic lifeline by accounting for up to 90 per cent of North Korean trade and providing food and other types of aid (Kim 2017). Aware of which country was the main benefactor of North Korea, Kim visited Hu three more times in 2010–11 as his health deteriorated and he prepared to lay the groundwork for his son, Kim Jong-un, to take over from him. Even in his last days, Kim understood that securing China's support would go a long way in ensuring the continuation of his family's dynastic rule.

However, North Korea could not count on unconditional support from China and Russia as the two countries improved relations with the United States. To begin with, both Beijing and Moscow pressed Pyongyang to reach an agreement with Washington during the Six-Party Talks in which all of them participated. As the host, China, in particular, was keen in the talks being successful (Funabashi 2007). Furthermore, both Beijing and Moscow agreed to the UN Security Council, of which they are of course permanent members, imposing sanctions on Pyongyang as the Kim family conducted its series of nuclear tests (UN Security Council 2023b). This was a particularly important blow for Pyongyang, for these sanctions scared potential investors. Furthermore, upon taking office Xi Jinping became the first Chinese leader to visit

South Korea before going to North Korea and in fact showed no particular interest in meeting with Kim Jong-un. The years went by, and Xi and Kim did not find the time to meet each other.

The situation changed in the late 2010s, when diplomacy between the two Koreas and between North Korea and the United States took hold during the Moon and Trump presidencies. Xi invited Kim to China in March 2018, to ensure that he would be the first foreign leader to meet with the third member of his family to rule North Korea. Kim went back to China in May and June, following his summits with Moon and Trump, respectively, and in January 2019, right before his (unsuccessful) Hanoi summit with the US president. And in June Xi visited North Korea to meet with Kim in Pyongyang for the first time since he had become China's president (Sun 2023). In the meantime, Kim also met with Putin during a trip to Russia in 2019 (Song 2019). Beijing and Moscow also started to refuse to allow the UN Security Council to impose new rounds of sanctions on Pyongyang, while asking the United States to engage in diplomatic negotiations (Pacheco Pardo 2023a). China and Russia also continued to be North Korea's main economic benefactors, especially the former. In other words, North Korea's relations with China and Russia had reached their highest point since the youngest Kim had taken office.

As relations between the United States on the one hand and China and Russia on the other deteriorated during the late 2010s and, especially, early 2020s, North Korea started to lean more heavily on its formal ally (China) and its partner (Russia) to withstand US sanctions and other forms of pressure. Throughout the Covid-19 pandemic, North Korea closed its borders. But as the country tentatively started to reopen, it received economic support from China and Russia once more (Reuters 2023a, 2023b). This was crucial for Kim to continue to run his country's economy, which had been badly hit by the border closure related to the pandemic.

More tellingly, the Kim regime's behaviour during Russia's invasion of Ukraine clearly showed that Pyongyang was seeking to strengthen relations with Moscow and Beijing as its diplomatic relations with Washington, and Seoul, showed no signs of improvement. North Korea provided military assistance to Russia, and was one of a handful of countries siding with Moscow in UN votes condemning the war

(Pacheco Pardo & Kim 2023). In September 2023, Kim met Putin in Russia's Far East. This was the North Korean leader's first meeting with a foreign leader since the Covid-19 pandemic (Chae 2023a). It was followed by North Korea transferring more weapons to Russia to continue its war with Ukraine, including missiles (Song 2024). The United States, meanwhile, took the lead in providing diplomatic and military support to Ukraine, so Russia's invasion of Ukraine informally pitched Washington against Pyongyang. Furthermore, South Korea was one of the few Asian countries openly supporting Ukraine, including supplying military equipment via third countries such as Poland (Pacheco Pardo & Kim 2023a). Therefore, North Korea was also informally confronting the South.

Ultimately, North Korea has an interest in maintaining good relations with China and Russia as long as its relationship with the United States continues to be problematic. Despite its preference for *Juche*, North Korea needs the diplomatic support of these two permanent members of the UN Security Council to ensure a degree of international political backing. Furthermore, China has become North Korea's essential economic partner with Russia also providing a degree of economic support. This is crucial for the Kim family to continue to maintain power in North Korea. Therefore, there are good reasons why North Korea is likely to continue to rely on China and Russia for years to come as part of its strategy to deal with the United States and with Washington's ally and Pyongyang's nemesis, South Korea.

4

"Defeat" at the hands of South Korea

It was a hot and humid morning in Seoul. Kim Dae-jung came out of the main door of the Blue House, then the official residence of the president of South Korea, together with his wife, Lee Hee-ho. The two of them climbed into the presidential limousine. Their driver took them to Gimpo International Airport, then the main airport in Seoul and South Korea, while tens of thousands of South Koreans lined up the streets to bid them farewell. At the airport, Kim delivered a message to his fellow South Koreans: the date is 13 June 2000, and the South Korean president is about to fly to Pyongyang for a summit meeting with his North Korean counterpart, Kim Jong-il. This was to be the first inter-Korean summit since the partition of Korea into two. Following 52 years of formal separation after centuries of existence as a single country, it was a momentous occasion.

After a short flight from Seoul to Pyongyang, Kim Dae-jung and his delegation held a successful summit with Kim Jong-il and his officials. The South Korean president spent a total of three days in North Korea. Kim Jong-il treated his South Korean counterpart with great respect and spent significant time alone with him. The two Koreas issued the North–South Joint Declaration on 15 June, at the end of the summit. In the declaration, they promised to achieve reunification independently, to pursue it via a federation or confederation formula, to facilitate exchanges between families separated during the Korean War, to promote economic and other type of cooperation and to engage in dialogue to implement the points agreed. The declaration also included an invitation for Kim Jong-il to visit South Korea. South Koreans were ecstatic. Reconciliation between the two Koreas was at hand. Many thought that even reunification would follow in a relatively short period of time. And indeed, economic cooperation in the form of the Kaesong Industrial Complex and regular family exchanges ensued. So did political, economic, cultural and sports exchanges. While there is no way of knowing what ordinary North Koreans thought about the summit and declaration, we can assume that they too were hopeful that reunification may have soon beckoned.

Over two decades after the first inter-Korean summit, however, reunification certainly has not happened and even reconciliation has proved elusive. North Korea continues to see South Korea as a "puppet" under the control of its "master", the United States. But at the same time, the very existence of a South Korea that is home to a vibrant democracy, a thriving economy and a globally influential culture is a slap in the face to the dictatorial, repressive, poor and relatively isolated North Korea. Even the intermittent inter-Korean summits and exchanges between the two Koreas from 2000 onwards are to an extent based on a quid pro quo: South Korea pays and North Korea provides access to its leader, access to separated family members, cheap labour or something else that Seoul wants. It is a transactional relationship, which underscores that, ultimately, there is no competition between the two Koreas anymore: Pyongyang has been defeated by Seoul.

THE COLD WAR: THE BATTLE FOR RECOGNITION AS THE "REAL" KOREA

North and South Korea were born out of two battles: a domestic battle about the present and future of the country after 35 years of colonization and a then incipient international battle between US-led capitalism and Soviet-led communism. Arguably, the international battle was the most important in determining the division of Korea into North and South. After all, Koreans of different political persuasion sought to find ways to coexist following their country's independence from Japan in 1945. But neither the United States nor, especially, the Soviet Union were willing to allow Koreans to decide their fate at the risk of Korea becoming part of Washington's or Moscow's camp. Thus, the United States repressed communist and leftist groups in South Korea during the USAMGIK years. And the Soviet Union repressed conservative and religious groups in North Korea and, crucially, prevented UN-sponsored Korean Constitutional Assembly elections taking place in May 1948 from being held north of the 38th parallel. Thus, Korea's division was to a large extent the result of Cold War enmity between the two superpowers of the day.

In this respect, the situation in Korea mirrored the situation in other parts of the world. China, Germany and Vietnam were also divided nations that emerged during the Cold War years, with capitalism versus communism becoming the fault line dividing Taiwan from China, West from East Germany and South from North Vietnam, as was the case with South and North Korea. And similarly to these other cases, the ideological division concomitant to the struggle between capitalism and communism resulted in protracted conflict. In the case of Vietnam, this conflict ended with a "hot" war between North and South that the former won. In the case of Germany, the conflict finished when the West absorbed the East following its collapse. In the case or Korea and China, the conflict is yet to end and arguably remains "frozen" in time, dating back to 1948 and 1949, respectively – the years when the Koreas were founded and when the People's Republic of China was established. This underscores that the battle for recognition between South and North during the Cold War was not unique but rather the result of the circumstances of the time.

In the beginning, of course, North Korea tried to "solve" the conflict with its neighbour to the south by force. Kim Il-sung started to prepare for an invasion of South Korea as soon as North Korea was established and the United States announced that its troops would eventually withdraw from the South (Cumings 2010). And Kim would probably have been successful had the United States not intervened in support of South Korea shortly after the start of the Korean War. Similarly to the case of the two Vietnams, the North was stronger at the beginning of the war, had the support of a powerful communist backer and had a strong ideological commitment to its cause, at least in theory. Differently from Vietnam, however, the South also had a strong commitment to its cause and received the support of the United States right until the end of the war. This is why Kim failed where Ho Chi Minh and Le Duan, in the case of North Vietnam, would later succeed. Even if the situations in the Koreas and the Vietnams seemed similar, ultimately there were also differences because of the history of each of them as well the characteristics of their respective leaderships and populations.

In spite of the failure of his attempt to reunify Korea by force, Kim would not renounce military and violent means to destabilize South Korea. The late 1950s and, especially, 1960s were particularly volatile. Most strikingly, in January 1968 a 31-member North Korean commando unit infiltrated South Korea with orders to kill its president, Park Chung-hee, and other government officials. The commandos were only repelled around 100 metres away from the Blue House. In addition, in February 1958 North Korean agents hijacked a domestic Korean Air flight in South Korea and diverted the flight towards Pyongyang. Eight South Korean passengers were never returned. In December 1969, Pyongyang's agents again hijacked a domestic Korean Air flight on its way to Seoul. Eleven of the abducted South Koreans on board would never be returned either. In addition, several North Korean commandos sought to infiltrate South Korea, and throughout these years North Korean agents engaged in killings in the DMZ and on South Korean territory multiple times, and the North Korean navy launched occasional attacks on South Korea's own navy (Fischer 2007). In other words, Kim would pursue a policy that ensured that South Korean leaders and the country's population at large never felt safe from North Korean violence.

At the same time, North and South Korea engaged in a politico-diplomatic and economic competition. With regard to the former, the first competition arena was the UN. Neither of the two Koreas could join the organization, as the Soviet Union vetoed the South's membership bid and in return the United States did the same regarding potential North Korean membership. Thus, the South became an observer in 1948, with the North following suit in 1973 after China replaced Taiwan in the UN Security Council. Throughout the 1950s and right up until the end of the Cold War, the "Korean Question" was raised dozens of times at the UN regarding how to bring about the peaceful reunification of Korea.[1] The question allowed South Korea first and eventually the two Koreas to present their position to the UN General Assembly. The

1 As of 2024, the UN Digital Library holds over 1,100 records on the topic of the "Korean question" dating to the period 1947–2017; see https://digitallibrary.un.org.

organization therefore became a key arena for the two countries to present their respective positions to a global audience.

The politico-diplomatic competition between the two Koreas also extended to the global arena. Both Seoul and Pyongyang engaged in a race to receive diplomatic recognition from as many countries as possible. Western countries, in general, recognized Seoul but not Pyongyang, with communist countries, broadly speaking, taking the opposite position. Thus, the competition was most heated in the so-called Third World, which sought to strike a balance between the capitalist and communist camps. South and North Korea used economic carrots, military assistance and other incentives to gain recognition from countries across Africa, different parts of Asia and Latin America (Pacheco Pardo 2023c). Throughout the 1960s and 1970s, there was no clear "winner" from this competition. After all, neither of the two Koreas seemed to be more powerful than the other. For most countries caught in the middle of their diplomatic competition and with no particularly ideological affinity with one or the other, it did not make sense to put their eggs in one of the Korea's baskets just yet.

As for the economic competition between the two Koreas, industrialization and growth became yet another battlefield for the Kim regime to "fight" against the South. By the end of the Korean War, both Koreas could be described as postcolonial states under authoritarian regimes that were devastated and impoverished by years of Japanese colonial rule and a fratricidal war. Therefore, both Kim and his South Korean opponents – mainly Park Chung-hee in the case of South Korea – launched processes to quickly rebuild their respective country's economies and "prove" that their preferred economic system, whether communism or capitalism, was better. Throughout the 1960s, North Korea had the upper hand. Both Koreas registered impressive rates of economic growth, but North Korea's industrialization progressed more rapidly and the standard of living of its citizens seemed to be improving faster (Cha & Pacheco Pardo 2023). Back in the 1960s, astute observers of Korean Peninsula affairs would have probably seen a brighter economic future in the North than in the South.

Underpinning all of this was the ideological competition that could be traced back to the very division of Korea. Kim broadly adhered to the key tenets of communism even if mixed with his *Juche* ideology (see Chapter 2). Park, meanwhile, was an avowed capitalist even if not of the private sector-led variety, given the central role of the state in his economic growth strategy. Their ideological competition was mainly focused on economics, given that South Korea was no beacon for democracy during this period. And initially, the case of North Korea could be used by communists worldwide to underscore that their system seemed to be better at improving the lives of ordinary workers. In this sense, the South arguably was doing a disservice to the capitalist bloc in the early stages of its competition with the North.

As the international environment changed, so did North Korea's approach to its southern neighbour. As explained in Chapter 3, Nixon's visit to China in February 1972 to meet with Mao created a new geopolitical situation, especially in Northeast Asia. As a result, Park and Kim saw an opening to try to improve inter-Korean relations. On the one hand, the decision by their two patrons to establish diplomatic relations helped to reduce tensions between the capitalist and communist sides in the region. On the other hand, neither Seoul nor Pyongyang were consulted by Washington and Beijing, respectively, about their thoughts regarding US–China rapprochement. Plus, there was the threat that Washington and Beijing may decide to abandon their respective alliances with Seoul and Pyongyang if it suited their broader interests. In the specific case of South Korea, rapprochement with China had led the Nixon administration to agree to China taking Taiwan's seat as a permanent member of the UN Security Council. Plus, it should not be forgotten that the United States was also considering abandoning South Vietnam in the hope of reaching a peace deal with North Vietnam. Therefore, both hope and fear informed inter-Korean rapprochement.

The intelligence services of the two Koreas thus held secret negotiations, and within a few months they were able to reach an agreement; the first since the division of Korea. The North–South joint communiqué issued on 4 July 1972 established the three principles for Korean reunification that, in theory, continue to inform Pyongyang's and Seoul's reunification policy more than 50 years later: independence, peace and national unity.[2] Independence referred to the two Koreas pursuing reunification by themselves and without interference from

2 The July 4 South–North Joint Communique. 4 July 1972.

external powers, particularly the United States and China. Peace made reference to the two Koreas agreeing that reunification could only come through diplomacy and negotiations rather than through war. And national unity essentially meant that the two Koreas would have to agree on the formula for reunification, which should be mutually agreeable, including to the peoples of the two countries. In short, the two Koreas sought to avoid a new Korean war and the great powers deciding their fate once more, and committed to diplomacy and negotiations as the means to solve their division.

Initially, it seemed that the two Koreas were indeed seeking to change the way they approached their bilateral relationship. Dating back to August 1971, inter-Korean Red Cross talks had been taking place. These accelerated following the July 1972 joint communiqué, with a focus on the reunion of separated families from the two Koreas (Pacheco Pardo 2022). It seemed that Kim and Park were willing to allow for this humanitarian gesture to go ahead, which was a significant step for two leaders on opposite sides of the ideological spectrum and who quite rightly thought that this type of openness could affect their domestic standing. The relationship between the two Koreas therefore seemed to be moving away from confrontation and enmity.

Alas, the short-lived inter-Korean rapprochement was not to endure. The Red Cross talks broke down, and neither the North nor the South took any real steps to implement their joint communiqué. Hostilities restarted in 1973, with shootings resuming along the DMZ, North Korea engaging in a four-year-long provocation campaign on the West Sea and Kim sending new agents to infiltrate the South (Suh 1995). At the same time, North Korea formally joined the Non-Aligned Movement (see Chapter 3). With South Korea unable to join because of its (perceived) dependence on and satellite status to the United States, membership of the Non-Aligned Movement gave Pyongyang the platform to gain the moral high ground over Seoul in terms of its "independence" of action in the international arena. The North Korean propaganda machine could claim that South Korea remained a "puppet" of the United States, and that North Korea was the only one of the two Koreas truly representing a strong, independent Korea on the global stage.

However, the late 1970s was also the period during which the economic competition between the two Koreas started to see a clear winner:

the South. North Korea was becoming unable to maintain high rates of economic growth once the period of rapid post-Korean War industrialization had come to an end. In contrast, South Korea was slowly moving up the value-added chain under Park's guidance and with *chaebol*, or big conglomerates, such as Hyundai, LG, Samsung or SK starting to become competitive at the global level. South Korea's export-oriented model had the advantage of the country being part of the capitalist camp, with the United States, especially, and increasingly Japan and western Europe serving as both financing sources and markets. In contrast, the communist economic model espoused by the Soviet Union was starting to show its limits, with negative ramifications for other communist economies, including North Korea. By the late 1970s, China's new leader, Deng Xiaoping, had decided that this model was not working for his country and launched a process of reform and opening up as explained in Chapter 3. This model would make China one of the three biggest economies in the world in a period of only three decades. North Korea, however, did not follow suit. Thus, its economy went down Moscow's path rather than Beijing's, to its own detriment.

Throughout the 1980s, North Korea also started to lose the politico-diplomatic competition in which it was embroiled with South Korea. At the same time as the South Korean economy was becoming much bigger than North Korea's, China and other communist countries, such as those in central and eastern Europe, were looking at new investment sources and Gorbachev launched a process of détente with the United States as a well as a domestic reform process (*Perestroika*). South Korea therefore became an attractive potential partner for a growing number of countries from the communist bloc. This was especially noticeable in the case of China. In 1983, Deng sent a delegation to South Korea to negotiate the repatriation of a group of Chinese would-be defectors. This was the first time that an official Chinese delegation had set foot in South Korea since the inauguration of China itself in 1949 (Lee 1983). From then on, South Korea and China engaged in political exchanges from time to time. But more importantly, to underscore North Korea's loss of political weight in the communist bloc, by 1984 South Korea had already become a bigger trade partner for China than its neighbour to the north (Chung 1991). As Deng put it, for China it did not matter whether the cat was black or white as long as it caught mice. For Beijing,

Seoul was the best of the two Koreas when it came to "catching mice" and supporting its economic opening-up process.

Improving political relations between South Korea and China dealt North Korea another blow in 1986. Seoul was due to host the Asian Games, in preparation for its hosting of the Summer Olympic Games two years later. The Kim regime urged its fellow communist countries to boycott the games. All did, except for China. Improving economic and political relations as well as Beijing's position as host of the 1990 Asian Games informed its decision to attend the games. This would be followed by more devastating news for North Korea as the 1988 Summer Olympic Games approached. As explained in Chapter 3, both the Soviet Union and China made it clear that they would be participating in the games, even as North Korea urged the communist camp to adopt a new boycott. Cuba would be the only country to follow Pyongyang's call. Moscow's and Beijing's decision opened the doors for all other communist countries to also announce that they would take part in the games.

The Kim family seemed to be unsure as to how to act in the face of its losing battle with Seoul. For the most part, North Korea resorted to violence. In 1983, North Korean agents planted a bomb in Rangoon (later Yangon) to assassinate South Korean president Chun Doo-hwan during an official visit to Burma (later Myanmar). The bomb missed Chun, but 21 people died, including several ministers in the South Korean president's cabinet. In 1986, North Korean agents also planted a bomb in Gimpo Airport in central Seoul in the run-up to the Asian Games. Five people died and several more were injured. The following year, other North Korean agents placed a bomb on a Korean Air flight as the Summer Olympic Games were approaching. All crew and passengers died as a result of the explosion (Pacheco Pardo 2022). In short, North Korea engaged in a terrorism campaign against the South as the means to undermine a country that was becoming more successful in all fields.

There was, however, a brief period of rapprochement following the Rangoon bomb attack. As explained in Chapter 2, South Korea suffered devastating floods in 1984. Pyongyang offered to provide aid to Seoul. The Chun government accepted. And in addition to aid, the two Koreas decided to send cultural delegations to each other and to host the first inter-Korea family reunion since the Korean War (Cha & Pacheco Pardo 2023). The trips by the cultural delegations and the family exchanges were emotional occasions and considered a success. But neither Kim nor Chun was able to build on them. North Korea would turn to terrorism only a few months later. As Pyongyang was losing its battle with Seoul, Kim was unable to find a way to strengthen relations with the South or to use this as way to improve his own country's economic fate.

SOUTH KOREA'S SUCCESS: NORTH KOREA'S RESPONSES

On 16 December 1987, South Korea held its first truly free democratic election since 1960. The election came after years of domestic opposition to Chun's dictatorship, with student, worker, feminist, white-collar and religious groups and protesters forcing the dictator's hand. The election was a victory for the South Korean people, who were able to convince their leaders of the need for political change thanks to relentless protests and the leadership of opposition figures such as Kim Dae-jung and Kim Young-sam. Coming in the midst of the third wave of democratization sweeping East Asia, Latin America and western Europe, however, South Korea's democratization was not particularly remarkable by global standards. Yet it was clearly a victory in the battle by the Koreas for international recognition, since North Korea continued as a dictatorial regime while South Korea would go on to quickly consolidate a strong democracy that still continues. This way, political competition would become a new battlefield for the two Koreas to wage their war for recognition as the "true" Korea.

The date of 17 September 1988 was arguably more relevant in the realm of inter-Korean competition. On that day, newly elected president Roh Tae-woo inaugurated the Seoul Summer Olympic Games. The games had been awarded to South Korea in 1981, with Chun seeing their hosting as a way to show the economic progress of South Korea under dictatorial rule but also as a means to bolster the dictatorship itself. Instead, the games became a veritable coming out party for a South Korea that was (fairly) rich, (newly) democratic and, crucially, able to convene most countries around the world after the boycotts of the Moscow 1980 and Los Angeles 1984 Summer Olympic Games. In contrast to South Korea's transition to democracy only the year before, the 1988 Seoul games did serve to unambiguously put South Korea on the global map. Plus, South Korea used the games to present to the world both a modern image but also traditional Korean culture and elements: *Hangul*, the *hanbok*, taekwondo, etc. This way, South Korea became the purveyor of Korean culture in the eyes of the rest of the world, which dealt another blow to Pyongyang.

North Korea could not have been more furious. In addition to boycotting Seoul 1988, Pyongyang sought to outdo its neighbour. On 1 July 1989, Kim Il-sung himself inaugurated the 13th Festival of Youth and Students. The setting was the Rungrado Stadium, which North Korea had built specifically for the festival, as a way to upstage the Seoul Olympic Stadium. In fact, the stadium would go on to host the parades in honour of the Kim family for which North Korea would become famous (see Chapter 2). Back in 1989, the stadium hosted over 20,000 delegates (Holley 1989). This was more than double the almost 8,500 athletes taking part in the Seoul Olympic Games. Perhaps this was another "victory" for North Korea, which could claim that its convening power was greater than the South's.

Yet the World Festival of Youth and Students was certainly no match for the Olympic Games. First held in 1947, the festival had essentially become a propaganda tool for communist countries as part of the competition with their capitalist opponents. Students and other young people from across the world would congregate for several days for discussions, sports and other activities. In the case of the games in Pyongyang, they would extend for a total of eight days. Participants came from at least 170 countries, including the United States, western Europe and in one case – after a four-country, ten-day trip – South Korea (Holley 1989). The festival itself was successful from a North Korean perspective, with the Kim regime presenting a friendly face to youth from all over the world. But it could certainly not compete with the global impact and glamour of the Seoul games.

Furthermore, the festival bankrupted Pyongyang. The Kim regime spent somewhere between US$4 billion and US$9 billion in erecting up to 260 buildings for the festival in just two years. Perhaps if the Soviet Union and other communist regimes had not collapsed, North Korea could have counted on the generosity of its allies and partners to cover the costs of such a lavish occasion. But this is a counterfactual. The reality is that the timing of the festival resulted in a huge financial cost for

Pyongyang. Plus, North Koreans got to see first-hand that Westerners coming to their country did not seem to be poor, oppressed or living in far worse conditions than their "communist paradise". None of them decided to defect to the supposed paradise that North Korea was. In fact, their political leaders had given them the freedom to travel to North Korea, whereas North Koreans were not free to travel the world themselves. From this perspective, the festival had a further negative impact on North Korea.

With the collapse of communism, countries in the (former) Eastern bloc moved swiftly to improve diplomatic relations with South Korea, and, dealing with its own economic crisis, North Korea was caught off-guard. With regard to diplomacy, in 1989 Hungary became the first country in the Soviet orbit to establish diplomatic relations with South Korea. The Soviet Union was among several countries to follow suit, with most central and eastern European countries normalizing relations with Seoul within a two-year period. China would then establish relations with South Korea in 1992, and Vietnam followed in 1995 (Ministry of Foreign Affairs of the Republic of Korea 2023), despite remaining a communist country and having fought against South Korean forces taking part in the Vietnam War. For North Korea, the risk of being absorbed by the South in the same way that East Germany had been incorporated by West Germany was real and perhaps more so, as North Korea suffered the Arduous March in the mid-1990s (see Chapter 2). If South Korea had anything to fear from North Korea in the early 1990s, it was its sudden collapse and the huge human and economic costs that this would entail.

Therefore, North Korea turned to diplomacy. Serendipitously for Kim Il-sung, Roh Tae-woo had announced his *Nordpolitik* in 1988. With this process, Seoul wanted to improve inter-Korean relations via economic, cultural and people-to-people exchanges, leading to better political relations. At the same time, Roh encouraged the United States and Japan, in particular, to improve relations with North Korea. And the South Korean president also sought to improve relations with the communist bloc, which explains the rapid establishment of diplomatic relations with central and eastern European countries, plus the Soviet Union and China (Roh 1988). Roh understood that this process benefited the South more than the North, for after all its economy was much bigger, its global political standing was increasing as well and its process of democratization meant that there was no authoritarian regime to preserve. But *Nordpolitik* was also informed by Roh's honest belief that the two Koreas could improve their relations, reconcile and reunify as Cold War hostilities were coming to an end. Over the decades, successive conservative and liberal administrations in South Korea have pursued their own policies towards North Korea, but the idea that inter-Korean exchanges can lead to reconciliation and, in the future, reunification has remained a constant.

It is in the context of the end of the Cold War, North Korea's multiple weaknesses and Roh's *Nordpolitik* that Kim decided to pursue negotiations with South Korea. To begin with, Pyongyang agreed to join the UN simultaneously with Seoul. In September 1991, the two of them gained accession to the New York-based organization, as explained in Chapter 3. The Soviet Union and China had made it clear to North Korea that they would not veto South Korea's bid to join, as they had maintained they would do in the past (Pacheco Pardo 2023c). Engaged in diplomatic normalization processes with Seoul and hopeful of receiving South Korean investment, neither Moscow nor Beijing had any reason to continue to oppose South Korea's membership. North Korea, therefore, had no option but to follow suit. For even worse than accepting that the two Koreas were to join the UN would have been seeing the South doing so while the North was left out.

UN accession helped to facilitate inter-Korean diplomacy. Most notably, the two Koreas signed the Agreement on Reconciliation, Non-aggression and Exchanges and Cooperation between the South and the North in December 1991.[3] As the first agreement between the two countries since 1972, the deal reaffirmed the principles set out by the Park Chung-hee and Kim Il-sung governments almost two decades earlier. In addition, the Basic Agreement, as it came to be known, also established that the two Koreas recognized each other's systems. This was a diplomatic victory for Kim, at a time when many thought that East Germany's past was North Korea's (impending) future. In a sense, Seoul was reassuring Pyongyang that it was not seeking to absorb North

3 Agreement on Reconciliation, Non-aggression and Exchanges and Cooperation between the South and the North. 13 December 1991.

Korea. Certainly, the South had its doubts about reunification because of the probable costs, but there is no doubt that Seoul would have stepped in and taken over North Korea had the latter dissolved.

Shortly afterwards, the two Koreas signed the Joint Declaration of the Denuclearization of the Korean Peninsula in January 1992. The agreement committed the two Koreas not to develop nuclear weapons.[4] It came in the context of the United States having removed its last nuclear warheads from South Korea the previous December, as part of a policy pursued by George H. W. Bush's administration to drastically reduce the number of Washington's nuclear weapons across the world. The agreement also took place in the context of North Korea having signed but not ratified the NPT a few years earlier. Thanks to this agreement, the two Koreas in theory committed to a nuclear-free Korean Peninsula. This was an essential confidence-building measure for North Korea, which for decades had felt threatened by the presence of US nuclear weapons in the South and now had no Soviet Union or China to rely on for its own security anymore.

Yet this period of diplomacy was short-lived. North Korea initiated the first nuclear crisis (see Chapter 5). Once the crisis seemed resolved, Pyongyang was in the midst of the Arduous March, which made the country turn inwards. At the same time, there were inter-Korean military clashes in 1996 and again in 1997. And in 1999, North Korean ships crossed the Northern Limit Line (NLL) separating the two Koreas at sea and clashed with the South Korean Navy in the first Battle of Yeonpyeong. At least 17 North Korean soldiers died during the battle (Pacheco Pardo 2023c). This demonstrated that neither international isolation following the end of the Cold War nor domestic economic problems would prevent the Kim family from engaging in violence against the South if it suited its interests.

At the same time, and somewhat paradoxically, North Korea also continued to seek diplomacy and engagement with South Korea throughout this period. To begin with, Seoul offered food aid to Pyongyang during the famine in the mid-1990s. North Korea gladly accepted this aid, which, pointedly, the South offered bilaterally rather than via the World

4 Joint Declaration of the Denuclearization of the Korean Peninsula. 20 January 1992.

Food Programme, which most countries supporting the North were using to channel their aid (Cha & Pacheco Pardo 2023). In addition, South Korea also joined the Korean Peninsula Energy Organization (KEDO) set up to provide North Korea with two light water reactors in exchange for its denuclearization (KEDO 2024). KEDO was launched as a result of the Agreed Framework signed by the United States and North Korea in 1994 (see Chapter 3). South Korea's membership of KEDO meant that it would provide financial and material support to the North. Shortly after, the two Koreas plus the United States and China launched the Four-Party Talks (US Department of State 1998). The Clinton administration was looking at ways to implement other aspects of the Agreed Framework, and multilateral rather than bilateral talks were more politically palatable to US Congress. Crucially, though, North Korea implicitly recognized the South as a dialogue partner in its negotiations with the United States. In the past, Pyongyang had demanded bilateral negotiations with Washington to discuss security matters, excluding Seoul. After all, the United States was the North's counterpart in the 1953 armistice and from Pyongyang's perspective the South was merely a "puppet" of its American master.

Engagement between the two Koreas reached new heights after Kim Dae-jung became South Korea's president in February 1998. Kim's Sunshine Policy called for engagement with the North, as previous South Korean policies had done. But Kim was a liberal with a decades-old track record of opposition to South Korea's earlier dictators and to its conservative politicians following democratization. Plus, the Sunshine Policy was not merely a campaign promise from Kim. The new South Korean president had formulated his approach towards North Korea decades earlier. He thus had a long track record of seeking engagement and reconciliation with Pyongyang as a means to create the conditions for reunification. This set him apart from previous South Korean leaders.

Kim Jong-il reacted to Kim Dae-jung's olive branch in kind. The reasons why still remain unclear. Perhaps the new North Korean leader genuinely wanted to improve relations with South Korea. After all, the North Korean leader was not responsible for the division of Korea into two or for having initiated the Korean War, as was the case with his father. Perhaps Kim saw in South Korean investment the solution to his country's economic problems and the key to unlocking economic reform. Or perhaps Kim simply wanted to ensure the survival of his family at the helm in North Korea, and engagement with the South was a means to prevent a South Korean takeover, a domestic revolution or both. Regardless of the reasons, the late 1990s and early 2000s were the heyday of inter-Korean engagement.

In November 1998, North Korea opened Mount Kumgang to tourism from the South. Widely regarded as the most beautiful mountain in the whole of the Korean Peninsula, tourists travelling from South Korea were allowed to travel to the North for leisure for the first time (Sims 2000). In June 2000, Kim Dae-jung and Kim Jong-il held the historic first inter-Korean summit after the South Korean president travelled to Pyongyang. The two Koreas signed a joint statement reiterating their wish to pursue reunification peacefully and independently, once again implicitly showing their respect for each other's system.[5] Following from the summit, Pyongyang agreed to inter-Korean family reunions for the first time since 1985. They became a regular feature throughout the 2000s (Ministry of Unification of the Republic of Korea 2021). And in 2004, the two Koreas opened the Kaesong Industrial Complex. This was the first inter-Korean economic project in history, matching capital, technology and know-how from the South with labour from the North. It would become the biggest symbol of inter-Korean cooperation over the following decade (Kim & Im 2009). Furthermore, in 2002 the second Battle of Yeonpyeong took place as once more North Korean ships crossed the NLL. But this time, in contrast to the first battle, Pyongyang quickly apologized for the clashes (Macfie 2010).

Yet North Korea continued to feel threatened by the South. *Hallyu*, or the Korean Wave, was taking East Asia first and the rest of the world next by storm. And it reached the North via smuggled movies, dramas and pop music. The *jangmadang* that had spread throughout the country became the main venue for South Korean cultural products to make their way throughout the country. North Koreans were attracted to the storylines, which reached their hearts and minds more easily than North Korean propaganda, and also to the visuals. This meant that many North Koreans found it easier to relate to South Korean movies,

5 South–North Joint Declaration. 15 June 2000.

dramas and songs depicting everyday life rather than their country's own propaganda about struggle, enemies and daily life stories that did not match their own experiences. Indeed, North Koreans could see a rich and modern country just south of the 38th parallel (Pacheco Pardo 2013). The number of defectors from North to South thus increased throughout the 2000s (Ministry of Unification of the Republic of Korea 2023a). Plus, North Koreans adopted the fashion, hairstyles, language and mannerisms coming from the South. The Kim regime launched regular crackdowns on South Korean culture, reportedly including public executions, but it was unable to stop the flow (Demick 2010). Similarly to *Hallyu* consumers in other parts of the world, North Koreans found South Korean cultural products irresistible.

Inter-Korean relations deteriorated again as a result of this "threat", North Korea's nuclear programme, the change in government in the South when the conservatives returned to power and the transition from Kim Jong-il to his son Kim Jong-un in the North. Roh Moo-hyun, South Korea's second liberal president after Kim Dae-jung, held a second inter-Korean summit with Kim Jong-il in October 2007 and even delivered a speech at a packed Rungrado Stadium (Ministry of Unification of the Republic of Korea 2021). But the conservative Lee Myung-bak took office in February 2008, and inter-Korean relations rapidly nosedived as the new South Korean president demanded more reciprocity from the North in return for his country's support (Moon 2011). Also, it was becoming more difficult for the South to justify engagement with the North after Pyongyang's first nuclear test in October 2006 (see Chapter 5). This was in direct contravention of the 1992 nuclear deal between the two Koreas. Thus, Lee suspended tours to Mount Kumgang shortly after taking office after a North Korean soldier shot a South Korean tourist and the Kim regime refused to apologize or to allow a joint investigation (Ministry of Unification of the Republic of Korea 2021). Also, in 2010 there were two new inter-Korean clashes. First, a North Korean torpedo sank ROKS *Cheonan*, killing 46 South Korean sailors (Moon 2011). Later in the year, the North Korean military shelled Yeonpyeong Island, killing four South Koreans including civilians (Moon 2011). Relations between the two Koreas hit rock bottom. In 2016, Park Geun-hye, the second consecutive conservative South Korean president following Lee and also daughter of Park Chung-hee, closed the Kaesong Industrial

Complex after North Korea's fourth nuclear test (Ministry of Unification of the Republic of Korea 2021). Both Lee and Park remained open to inter-Korean dialogue, but North Korea seemed to only be interested in it if there were no demands to give something in return.

With Kim Jong-un in power, relations between the two Koreas thus were almost non-existent during the conservative administrations of Lee and Park. The situation changed dramatically after the liberal Moon Jae-in took office in May 2017. Moon became president shortly after Donald Trump took office in the United States. The South Korean president had worked under Roh Moo-hyun, including during the organization of his 2007 inter-Korean summit, and was keen on engagement with North Korea as a way to bring reconciliation between the two Koreas. The US president, meanwhile, believed in his power of persuasion to convince Pyongyang to give up its nuclear weapons. The conditions were thus ripe for diplomacy on the Korean Peninsula once again. Moon invited North Korea to participate at the PyeongChang Winter Olympic Games scheduled for February 2018. In contrast to Seoul 1988, 30 years later North Korea attended PyeongChang 2018. What is more, Kim Yo-jong, the sister of Kim Jong-un, led the North's delegation (Yonhap 2018). She was the first member of the Kim family to step on South Korean soil since at least the Korean War.

PyeongChang 2018 opened the door to a period of dramatic diplomatic engagement. In April, Moon and Kim Jong-un held the first inter-Korean summit in 11 years. I was in Seoul at the time, and it was clear that there was as a sense of scepticism mixed with excitement. After all, on the one hand there had already been two summits but on the other hand Kim Yo-jong had caused a great impression during her February visit. The sense of excitement ultimately prevailed on the day. This started when Moon and Kim Jong-un held hands on the DMZ, Moon briefly crossed into the North's side, and Kim then became the first leader of the North to set foot in the South again since at least the Korean War (Berlinger & Hancocks 2018).[6] At the time, the summit was considered a success even if the joint statement issued was not

6 To this day, it is not settled whether Kim Il-sung crossed the 38th parallel or not during the Korean War, as North Korean troops made their way through South Korea.

necessarily pathbreaking. Furthermore, Moon and Kim met at short notice the following month. This was a first in the history of inter-Korean relations. Rather than a carefully orchestrated and choreographed summit, the leaders of the two Koreas had a phone call and decided to meet within a few hours (Haas & Gambino 2018). Following the summit between Trump and Kim in Singapore (see Chapter 3), Moon went to North Korea in September. There he became the first South Korean president to visit Mount Paektu, and he was also invited to deliver a speech at Rungrado Stadium, as his mentor, Roh Moo-hyun, had done 11 years earlier (Lee 2018). Perhaps secure in power now that his country was a full-fledged nuclear power, Kim wanted to focus on the other line included in *byungjin*: economic development. South Korean investment could be key.

At the time, I had the chance to meet North Korean officials several times, always in different locations. One conversation particularly struck me. A North Korean official spent the dinner asking questions, in Korean, about life in South Korea in general and Seoul in particular. They were eager to absorb as much information as possible, and to get an understanding about how life in South Korea compared to the country in which we were meeting, as well as my own home country (Spain). As curious as I was about life in North Korea, they were curious about life in the country that, in theory, was their enemy. This North Korean official expressed hope that the improvement in inter-Korean relations at the time would perhaps allow them to eventually learn more about the South. Human curiosity, it seemed, trumped decades of propaganda about the "evil" country below the 38th parallel.

Alas, this was not to be. Inter-Korean relations could not progress as US–North Korea diplomacy stalled. The North Korean regime went back to hurling insults at the South, including at Moon himself. The Covid-19 pandemic then provided Kim with the perfect reason to cease contact with the South. By the time North Korea was ready to reopen in 2023, the conservative Yoon Suk-yeol had become South Korea's new president. North Korea showed no interest in engaging in dialogue with the Yoon government. In fact, the Kim regime even increased pressure on its own population to stop the spread of South Korean culture across North Korea. Most notably, Kim implemented a ban on the use of South Korean expressions in early 2023 (Mun 2023). After decades of division, the Korean used in North and South had diverged, with the version used in the latter becoming more informal. A growing number of North Koreans preferred this, especially younger ones (Demick 2010; Mun 2023). Even this was a threat for the Kim family.

In fact, in January 2024 Kim Jong-un called for South Korea to be labelled as the North's "primary foe and invariable principal enemy" in its constitution. He also called for Pyongyang to move away from concepts such as "reunification", "reconciliation" and "fellow countrymen", while ordering the dismantling of North Korean agencies tasked with promoting inter-Korean relations (Kim 2024). Seemingly, the two Koreas had become separate entities from Kim's perspective. In a sense, this implicitly recognized that the economically backward, nuclear-armed North Korea was fundamentally different from the vibrant and developed South Korea. Hence, reunification under anything resembling North Korean terms was essentially unthinkable. It could be said that its "defeat" at the hands of the South was now almost complete.

THE VIEW FROM THE SOUTH: A POOR, MAD "BROTHER"?

South Koreans' perceptions of North Korea have naturally evolved over time. A key reason behind this change has unsurprisingly been the different position of the South vis-à-vis the North. In the years following the division of Korea and the Korean War, the two Koreas were in a relatively similar position. It would have been difficult to predict which one of the two would come on top, if any, and in any case the expectation was that reunification would take place in a relatively short period of time. It was a vision of inter-Korean relations still strongly influenced by *minjok*, the idea of Korea's distinct identity described previously. Thus, it was not only necessary but also natural that the two Koreas would once again become one. It was therefore necessary to develop a strong South Korea, not only for the sake of South Koreans themselves but also for the sake of their sisters and brothers in the North.

At the same time, nonetheless, it was crucial to ensure that reunification would happen in accordance with Seoul's own terms. Especially for the leaders of South Korea and the many Koreans who had decided to settle in the South following the Korean War, it was necessary to create an advanced nation (*Seonjinguk*) that would be strong enough to prevent an invasion from the North and a revolution from within (Park 1976). This was a crucial reason why South Korea needed economic development but also a reason to keep the South Korea–US alliance. It was also the justification given to engage in domestic repression. From this perspective, anyone espousing communist sympathies was a potential threat: a fifth column that could be used by the Kim family to bring communism to South Korea.

Therefore, it is fair to say that most South Koreans saw the North as a potential threat from the 1950s to the 1970s (Cha & Pacheco Pardo 2023). Memories from the Korean War were fresh. Repression and censorship ensured that South Koreans were predetermined, or forced, to see North Korea in a particular (i.e. negative) way. There were also of course inter-Korean clashes, especially across the DMZ, infiltrations by North Korean commandos, assassination attempts of South Korean leaders and the broader context of the global battle between capitalism and communism that informed the Cold War and underpinned a negative attitude towards North Korea. Neither domestic nor international conditions were conducive for South Koreans developing positive views of North Korea.

Yet South Korea was not prey to monolithic thinking even during the worst years of dictatorial repression. Throughout the 1950s and 1960s, protests against the government regularly called for reunification. In fact, Park Chung-hee's 1961 coup was partly related to demands for immediate reunification, at least among the protesters who had forced Rhee Syngman's resignation. The student movement, in particular, made this a centrepiece of its platform. After all, many harboured communist sympathies at a point when it was not clear that capitalism was a better economic system for developing countries to adopt (Pacheco Pardo 2022). Plus, many South Koreans felt that the division of Korea had been decided by the big powers and that the political weakness of their country as embodied by their leaders was also to blame. They wanted to restore the historical state of affairs: a single Korea with its territory encompassing the whole of the Korean Peninsula.

Concurrently, there were hundreds of thousands of South Koreans whose families had been divided as a result of the Korean War, and who did not want this situation to continue indefinitely. These families also wanted reunification, whether for these personal reasons or for a mixture of personal reasons as well as the belief that the government, at least partially, was to blame for the division of Korea (Kim 2016). In spite of the repression and authoritarianism inherent to the Park Chung-hee dictatorship, these families were a force to be reckoned with because their push for reunification did not stem from any particular ideology but rather from the very human desire to meet and reunite with their loved ones. The government could not simply ignore their plight and label them as communist sympathizers who posed a threat to the very existence of South Korea.

And let's not forget, Park's official position was that the ultimate goal of his government was reunification. The South Korean president presented himself as the only person who could bring about reunification on South Korean terms, along with a prosperous and powerful (South) Korea (Park 1976). But whereas Rhee thought that reunification was possible by force back in the 1950s, Park had a more realistic approach to inter-Korean relations. This helps to explain why his government signed the 1972 agreement with North Korea. It was an acknowledgement that reunification could only come via dialogue and negotiations, barring the collapse of one of the regimes.

Throughout the 1970s and, especially, 1980s, the groups wary of a communist takeover (mainly conservative) and the groups demanding reunification (mainly liberal) continued their confrontation. But the latter became more vocal in linking dictatorship with the impossibility of moving ahead with reunification. The *minjung* movement that came to dominate opposition to the Park and Chun Doo-hwan regimes linked their dictatorial rule to the United States, which many believed was responsible for the (unnatural) division of Korea. This movement also blamed the Park and Chun regimes for the reality that reunification was becoming ever more difficult as time passed (Lee 2007). In response, Park and Chun doubled down on warnings that, in their view, South Koreans calling for an end to their dictatorial rule in reality were communists who essentially wanted the South to fall to the North (Shin & Hwang 2003). Most infamously, Chun blamed the Gwangju Uprising of May 1980, arguably South Korea's best-known protest against dictatorship, on communist sympathizers and North Korean agents (Shin & Hwang 2003). In this sense, there were two different views of North

Korea: a hostile threat with which to eventually reunify under a powerful South Korea and a "brother" with which to reunify as soon as possible.

The late 1980s and early 1990s marked an inflexion point in South Korean perceptions of North Korea. To begin with, there was an obvious change in the relative position of the South vis-à-vis the North. As already explained, by the 1980s South Koreans were becoming aware that their country was richer and more developed than the North. Then came the transition to democracy in 1987–8, immediately followed by Seoul hosting the 1988 Olympic Games. South Korea was becoming freer and more international, while the North was seemingly stuck in the past. In the minds of many South Koreans, the death of Kim Il-sung in 1994, Pyongyang's nuclear sabre rattling, and news of the famine that struck North Korea in the mid-1990s only served to confirm that their neighbour was no match for modern South Korea.

At the same time, South Korea underwent a process of internationalization that also changed its position globally. From the 1980s onwards, travel restrictions were relaxed and a growing number of South Koreans were able to travel overseas for tourism, study and work, rather than as poor migrants moving to richer countries. Meanwhile, South Korean *chaebol* were now becoming global firms driven by innovation rather than the manufacture of cheaper versions of American, European or Japanese products. Plus, membership of the UN gave an impulse to South Korean global standing as the country became an active diplomatic actor in areas ranging from peacekeeping to climate change discussions. And from the 1990s, South Korea started to become internationally recognized for its modern culture thanks to *Hallyu* or the "Korean Wave", which served to attract a growing number of tourists to South Korea, especially from the early 2000s onwards (Kim & Nam 2016).

The shifting balance of power between the two Koreas, and South Korea's internationalization, resulted in a change in mentality among South Koreans. Civic nationalism became the main driver of the meaning of what being South Korean was, according to most South Koreans themselves (Kim 2006b). Essentially, this meant that membership of the South Korean polity by respecting and contributing to the society, politics and economy of the country became the central factor in determining whether one was considered to be part of it or not. *Minjok* of course continued to inform South Koreans' perception of themselves and their relationship with the rest of the world. But *minjok* no longer exercised a monopoly over South Korean identity , and for younger South Koreans it became secondary to civic nationalism (Kim 2006b). An increasing number of South Koreans felt closer to their fellow citizens in developed countries than to North Koreans.

This shift inevitably affected relations with North Korea. A majority of South Koreans continued to believe that reunification between the two Koreas is necessary. But a growing number of younger South Koreans disagreed with the need for reunification, whether because of its economic costs or a lack of affinity with the Kim family and its dictatorship (Kim *et al.* 2014). Certainly, this needs to be qualified. It is one thing for someone asked by a pollster to express their opposition to reunification when this prospect seems distant at best. It would be different for a South Korean to answer the same question if, for example, there was a process of reconciliation laying the groundwork for reunification, or if the North Korean regime collapsed and South Korea faced the dilemma of either absorbing the North or living with a failed – or Chinese-controlled – neighbour. It is probable that most South Koreans would choose the first option. And yet, it has to be acknowledged that reunification is not a priority for most South Koreans.

Yet reunification does continue to be a priority for any South Korean president and the country's political elites more generally. Dating back to Roh Tae-woo and all the way to Yoon Suk-yeol, all South Korean presidents have launched a North Korean policy that, in their view, would help create the conditions for reunification to eventually take place. Plus, all South Korean presidents since democratization have been open to holding a summit with their North Korean counterpart (Cha & Pacheco Pardo 2023). After all, if (or when) reunification takes place, the South Korean president who achieves it will go down in the history books. So South Korean presidents have a personal incentive to pursue reunification, beyond the broader interests of their country and the long history of Korea as a single entity. And without having to resort to being cynical, most South Koreans continue to believe that theirs is an artificially divided country, a belief shared by South Korean presidents.

Over time and after more than 35 years of democracy, it seems that, generalizing, two main visions of reunification have emerged among South Korean leaders and their followers. The "liberal" view is based on the idea that reconciliation should precede reunification. From this perspective, the two Koreas have grown too far apart. Thus, it is necessary to promote civil society exchanges, economic cooperation and elite meetings for the purpose of trust-building. Creating these links will make North Korean leaders and the population more conformable with a process of opening up to the rest of the world. This way, the two Koreas will be laying the foundations for future generations to bring about peaceful reunification. This vision does not mean abandoning the deterrence of a nuclear-armed North Korea or naively believing that the Kim family has altruistic reasons to abandon over 75 years of dictatorship. But the goal is to change the calculus of Pyongyang so that reunification becomes realistic (Cha & Pacheco Pardo 2023).

The "conservative" view, for its part, stresses that it is the duty of any South Korean president to prepare for reunification. Preparations include creating a strong South Korea so that North Korea feels compelled to negotiate. Deterrence and a strong South Korea–US alliance are quintessential to this vision, as it forces a change in calculus from Pyongyang so that the Kim family realizes that it is in its own interest to move towards reconciliation with the South. This vision, meanwhile, believes that engagement should be predicated on reciprocity. In other words, the (stronger) South and the (weaker) North should have economic, political and civil society exchanges. But North Korea should make political concessions to the South in exchange for Seoul's largesse. At the very least, North Korea should commit to denuclearization and refrain from missile tests and military provocations and propaganda against the South. Eventually, the conditions will be set for reunification (Cha & Pacheco Pardo 2023).

The differences between liberals and conservatives when it comes to reunification should not be overemphasized. Most notably, recent conservative and liberal leaders have sought to shift the debate from the costs of reunification to its potential benefits. Following from Germany's reunification, a growing number of South Koreans became alarmed at the cost that West Germany bore as it absorbed East Germany. It is estimated that Germany spent US$2 trillion in upgrading and modernizing the East's infrastructure, providing jobs and education to the East German population and on direct economic transfers to close the gap between the incomes in both countries (Gumbel 2009). And North Korea's economy is much smaller than South Korea's in 2024. The gap between the two Koreas is far wider than that between West and East Germany when the two countries reunified in 1990 (Lee & McKibbin 2018). From the perspective of many South Koreans, the prospect of absorbing and modernizing North Korea looks terrifying.

Yet both the conservative Park Geun-hye (2013) and the liberal Moon Jae-in (2017) referred to the benefits of reunification as much as its costs. The most obvious benefit would be the peace dividend that would come from the two Koreas being able to reduce their militaries. At 2.7 per cent of GDP, South Korea's military budget is one of the largest in the world in relative terms (International Institute for Strategic Studies 2023). In the case of North Korea, there are no accurate figures, but it is estimated that the Kim family spends up to 25 per cent of the country's GDP on its armed forces (International Institute for Strategic Studies 2023). A unified Korea could thus free up tens of billions of dollars to spend on welfare, infrastructure development or any other area. In addition, it is widely believed that geopolitical instability reduces investment in South Korea. Plus, South Korea's stock exchange is undervalued as a result of inter-Korean tensions (Kim 2018). In addition, the reconstruction of North Korea would open up investment opportunities and jobs for South Korean firms and workers (Song *et al.* 2019). Plus, a unified Korea would be connected to the Eurasian landmass in a way that South Korea currently is not, since the very existence of North Korea has essentially transformed the South into an island. This would bring further economic benefits, such as new land routes for trade. And at a personal and human level, reunification would of course allow families separated by the Korean War and their descendants to reunite. The point that Park and Moon made was not that reunification would not be costly. It would. Their point was that the benefits, including economic ones, outweigh the costs.

Other than reunification, Pyongyang's nuclear weapons is another key issue that preoccupies South Korean leaders. From time to time, it also occupies the minds of the general population. But as any resident in or visitor to South Korea can attest, South Koreans are blasé about the risk of nuclear war on the Korean Peninsula. South Korea has been living under the shadow of the North Korean military threat too long for South Koreans to worry about it on a daily basis. Yet their leaders are preoccupied with how to deter a North Korean nuclear attack and, if at all possible, how to bring about the denuclearization of North Korea (Cha & Pacheco Pardo 2023). Deterrence is part of South Korea's strategy, which helps to explain why South Korean leaders want a strong South Korean army to supplement the South Korea–US alliance, which no South Korean president questions (Snyder 2018). North Korea's possession of nuclear weapons has also opened a debate in the South about the possibility of the country developing nuclear warheads of its own. Certainly, South Korea could develop nuclear weapons relatively quickly and, most probably, with no major backlash, at least from the United States and other Western countries (Pacheco Pardo 2023b). For the time being, however, deterrence is the main way in which Seoul confronts Pyongyang's nuclear weapons.

And then there is the issue of North Korea's human rights abuses. South Korea's rapid democratic consolidation and strong civic nationalism mean that a majority of South Koreans abhor the way in which the Kim family abuses the human rights of the North Korean population (Ministry of Unification of the Republic of Korea 2023b). During the Park Geun-hye government, the South Korean National Assembly even passed a human rights act calling out the Kim regime for its poor human rights record and for South Korea to support the victims of the regime.[7] South Korea has also joined UN votes denouncing Pyongyang's human rights record (UN 2022, 2023b). Unsurprisingly, North Korea has hit back and denounced South Korea's focus on its human rights situation, pointing the finger at Seoul's own alleged human rights abuses (KCNA 2011, 2013b). And in private meetings, North Korean officials have justified these abuses by pointing out that their country technically remains at war with the United States and needs to "protect" itself against domestic sources of instability. Yet these explanations do not cut it in South Korea.

All in all, South Koreans' views of North Korea have transformed over time as their own country has changed over the decades. As of 2024,

7 North Korea Human Rights Act. 3 March 2016.

most South Koreans do not think about the North on a daily basis. They are busy with their own lives, which North Korea does not particularly affect. And when they think about North Korea, they are ambivalent about the country occupying the other half of the peninsula. When push comes to shove, it is likely that most of them would support reunification. Certainly, a large majority still wants reunification. But this is not the priority for South Koreans today as it was shortly after the partition of the country. South and North Korea are too different at the time of writing, and this shows in the way that Seoul relates to Pyongyang.

5

Becoming a nuclear power

The bombastic and exuberant Ri Chun-hee took to the television screens of North Koreans up and down the country on 3 September 2017. Dressed in a pink *hanbok* and wearing the obligatory badge with portraits depicting Kim Il-sung and Kim Jong-il, North Korea's most famous TV presenter had an announcement to make. It was to be a major announcement, for Ri, now in her seventies, was semi-retired and only appeared on the screen of her fellow North Koreans when there was big news to announce. And the news certainly merited Ri's presence: earlier that day, Pyongyang had conducted a hydrogen bomb test. This was North Korea's sixth nuclear test, with a blast between 70 and 280 kilotons. That is, at least three times bigger than the previous test and a whopping 100 times more powerful than North Korea's first nuclear test, conducted on 9 October 2006. Unsurprisingly, Ri was using the Kim family's propaganda platform to hail "a very meaningful step in completing the national nuclear weapons programme" (BBC 2017).

Leaders from across the world reacted to North Korea's sixth nuclear test as they had done with the previous five. As a case in point, US President Donald Trump tweeted "North Korea has conducted a major nuclear test. Their words and actions continue to be very hostile and dangerous to the United Nations" (Balluck 2017). Although using a different, undiplomatic medium to comment on the test compared to previous American presidents, Trump did not deviate from his predecessors when it came to substance. Shortly after the test, the UN Security Council slapped a new round of sanctions on North Korea. With little to show after more than a decade of incremental sanctions on the North Korean regime and economy, sanctions had nonetheless become the default option for the international community to show its opposition to Pyongyang's nuclear programme. At the same time, some voices called for the resumption of dialogue with the Kim regime to try to move North Korea in the direction of denuclearization. By September 2017, those arguing that only more sanctions or, conversely, more dialogue would put an end to North Korea's nuclear programme were firmly convinced that theirs was the best means to denuclearize the country.

The truth is that North Korea is a de facto nuclear power. De jure, the international community is unlikely to ever recognize Pyongyang's nuclear status. In practice, however, North Korea has been a nuclear state for almost 20 years, at the very least since it conducted its first nuclear test. And North Korea is unlikely to willingly denuclearize. After all, and in the view of the Kim regime, Hussein and Gaddafi were removed from power essentially because they gave up their weapons of mass destruction. Similarly, Russia invaded Ukraine only because the latter willingly surrendered the nuclear weapons left in its territory following the disintegration of the Soviet Union. And equally relevant, possession of a nuclear weapons programme has been the decades-long project of the Kim family, who see it as the ultimate deterrent against a possible US invasion as well as a source of prestige. For a country that is poor, repressive and decades behind South Korea, nuclear weapons at least confer a modicum of prestige on the global stage.

THE KIM FAMILY AND THE BOMB: BECOMING A NUCLEAR POWER

Kim Il-sung, Kim Jong-il and Kim Jong-un: three generations of North Korean leaders. Three generations of leaders obsessed with making North Korea a nuclear power. And decades of obsession have resulted in an undeniable success. As of 2024, North Korea is one of only nine countries to possess nuclear warheads. And is only one of four to successfully develop a nuclear weapons programme after the 1968 NPT barred all countries, except for the five original nuclear powers, from developing their own nuclear weapons. India, Israel and Pakistan are the three other countries to have defied the NPT and built their own nuclear arsenals since the treaty was launched. Membership of this exclusive club matters for North Korea. The fact that South Korea does not have nuclear warheads of its own, mainly for political rather than technological reasons, matters to Pyongyang as well. This is one of the few areas in which the Kim family can credibly argue that they are stronger than their neighbour.

North Korea's wish to develop its nuclear programme can be traced back to the aftermath of the Second World War and the Korean War. That is, this is a decades-old wish of the Kim family almost from the establishment of their country. North Korean leaders saw how Little Boy and Fat Man, the nuclear bombs that the US dropped over Hiroshima and Nagasaki, respectively, swiftly forced Japan to surrender to put an end to the Second World War. Then, North Korea saw how US support for South Korea prevented its victory in the Korean War. What is more, the United States carpet-bombed North Korea during the conflict and even considered dropping atomic bombs on the country (Cumings 2010). Arguably, Pyongyang had a compelling case to seek nuclear weapons.

In January 1958, the United States started to station nuclear warheads in South Korea (Kristensen & Norris 2017). North Korea's enemy was now undoubtedly covered by Washington's nuclear umbrella. Japan and Taiwan, the two other allies of the United States in Northeast Asia, were also de facto protected by its nuclear weapons (Roehrig 2017). In Northeast Asia, the Soviet Union of course was also a nuclear power since its first test in 1949. China was also developing its own nuclear weapons and would go on to conduct its first test in 1964. From a purely nuclear weapons perspective, North Korea was the odd one out. Pyongyang would technically be protected by the nuclear weapons programme of the Soviet Union and China after it signed defence treaties with both of them in 1961, but the fact was that North Korea was located in one of the most nuclearized regions in the world. This helped to further fuel the Kim family's nuclear ambitions.

In fact, North Korea's position was similar to that of countries in the Middle East or in South Asia. In the case of the Middle East, Israel started to develop its own nuclear programme in the late 1940s and would go on to have all the necessary components to build nuclear weapons by the late 1960s (Farr 1999). Israel's neighbours, including Iran, Libya and Syria, felt threatened by its nuclear programme and also sought to acquire their own nuclear warheads. In the case of South Asia, India conducted its first nuclear test in 1974 after also starting its nuclear programme in the 1940s. Pakistan then accelerated its own nuclear programme after India's test, conducting its first full test in 1998 (Khan 2008). And let's not forget, the United Kingdom conducted its first nuclear test in 1952 and France followed suit in 1960. Even if both were formal treaty allies with the United States following the launch of NATO in 1949, and in spite of US leaders deploying nuclear weapons in Europe from the mid-1950s, London and Paris only felt safe from the Soviet nuclear threat with their own warheads. In other words, already by the late 1950s North Korea was facing the same security dilemma that fellow would-be nuclear powers in different parts of the world were also mulling.

Thus, Pyongyang asked Moscow to help in the development of its own nuclear weapons. Soviet leaders refused, but the two sides signed a nuclear cooperation agreement in 1959 whereby the Soviet Union agreed to continue to provide training to North Korean nuclear scientists, which had already started a few years earlier, to deploy its own scientists in North Korea and to transfer technology to develop nuclear facilities (Clemens 2010). This way, the Soviet Union would help North Korea to kick-start a civilian nuclear energy programme. As early as 1962, North Korea opened the Yongbyon nuclear facility in North Pyongan Province, in North Korea's northwest. This facility would eventually come to symbolize Pyongyang's nuclear weapons programme. Back in the 1960s, North Korea also started to lay the groundwork for the mining operations that would allow it to extract the uranium on which its nuclear programme was to be based (Clemens 2010).

The Kim family only fully revived its nuclear weapons ambitions in the early 1980s, once Kim Jong-il was safely confirmed as the heir to his father Kim Il-sung. It was during these years that North Korea started to expand the Yongbyon nuclear facility while at the same time accelerating development of a domestic plutonium production programme (Mack 1993). There are credible reports that China assisted North Korea throughout the decade, providing technical assistance and weapons-grade uranium that North Korea could use to pursue a nuclear weapons programme using this element rather than plutonium (Plant & Rhode 2013). Furthermore, North Korea conducted its first known missile tests in 1984 (CSIS 2022). Launched in the late 1970s, Pyongyang's missile programme – based on the Scud-B developed by the Soviet Union and acquired by the Kim regime from Egypt – allowed North Korea to boost its deterrence capabilities (Potter & Stulberg 1990). But missiles could also serve to mount miniaturized nuclear warheads that could then be fired from one's own country, without the need for a bomber to fly over to drop the warhead. In this sense, North Korea's quest for nuclear weapons and development of a missile programme became intertwined throughout the 1980s.

The Soviet Union became aware of North Korea's nuclear weapons programme at a time when Mikhail Gorbachev, the country's newly inaugurated leader, was seeking a thaw in relations with the United States. Moscow thus cajoled Pyongyang into joining the NPT, which it did in December 1985 (IAEA 2023). NPT membership, however, did not put an end to Kim Il-sung's nuclear ambitions. The North Korean leader refused to sign a safeguards agreement with the International Atomic Energy Agency (IAEA), a necessary step for the agency to be able to carry out inspections of North Korea's nuclear facilities to ensure compliance with the NPT. Plus, Yongbyon's first nuclear reactor became operational in 1986 (Mack 1993). At best, North Korea was only half-heartedly showing its potential willingness to halt its nuclear weapons programme. With hindsight, we now know that the Kim family was bent on acquiring its own warheads.

The late 1980s and early 1990s were a time of geopolitical change with the collapse of the Soviet Union and the end of the Cold War. At the same time, China was embarked on its ongoing process of economic opening up. These changes seem to have convinced the Kim family that only North Korea could provide for its own security. As a result, Pyongyang accelerated development of its nuclear and missile programme during this period of time. On paper, this was not the case. In December 1991, the George H. W. Bush administration removed all American nuclear weapons from South Korea as part of its worldwide withdrawal of naval and land-based tactical nuclear warheads (Kristensen & Norris 2017). Within weeks, the two Koreas agreed to the Joint Declaration on the Denuclearization of the Korean Peninsula. Signed in January 1992, the agreement committed the two Koreas not to manufacture or possess nuclear weapons and nuclear reprocessing and uranium enrichment facilities.[1] That same month, Pyongyang finally concluded a safeguards agreement with the IAEA. And in May 1992, North Korea allowed IAEA inspectors to visit the country to monitor compliance with the safeguards agreement (IAEA 2023). Yet North Korea had resumed its missile testing in 1990 (CSIS 2022). This was a sign that Pyongyang was looking into ways of boosting its security and defence capabilities.

The first North Korean nuclear crisis began in March 1993. In late 1992, IAEA inspectors asked for several clarifications from Pyongyang after they found a number of discrepancies between North Korea's initial report on its nuclear programme and the information that they had collected during their inspection. In early 1993, IAEA inspectors requested access to two sites where they believed North Korea was storing nuclear waste. The inspectors suspected that Pyongyang had not been keeping to its commitments under the NPT. North Korea declined the request, and the inspectors responded by reiterating it (Wit, Poneman & Gallucci 2004). The Kim regime and IAEA inspectors were now embroiled in a standoff.

North Korea then kick-started its first nuclear crisis by announcing its decision to withdraw from the NPT within three months, as per the treaty's provisions. A few weeks later, the IAEA announced that Pyongyang was non-compliant with its safeguards agreements. North Korea then suspended withdrawal from the NPT, as the Bill Clinton administration agreed to hold bilateral talks to defuse tensions and reach an agreement for North Korea to freeze and reverse its nuclear weapons programme. Washington and Pyongyang engaged in bilateral talks (Wit, Poneman & Gallucci 2004), which was a major diplomatic victory for the Kim family. Its nuclear threat had brought the world's superpower to the negotiation table. In October 1994, the Clinton administration and the Kims, now with Kim Jong-il at the helm after his father had passed away only a few weeks earlier, signed the Agreed Framework. In this agreement, North Korea agreed to freeze its nuclear weapons programme in return for the normalization of diplomatic relations and economic support. Herein was another lesson for North Korea: its nuclear programme could lead to concessions from the superpower as well.

1 Joint Declaration on the Denuclearization of the Korean Peninsula. 20 January 1992.

North Korea put an end to its plutonium programme. Unknown to most of the outside world, however, North Korea started to develop its highly enriched uranium (HEU) programme in earnest. In order to do so, North Korea could count on the help of another would-be nuclear power: Pakistan. In December 1993, Pakistani Prime Minister Benazir Bhutto visited North Korea, which accelerated cooperation between Pyongyang and Islamabad: the former provided missile components to the latter, and in exchange the latter offered nuclear know-how and uranium enrichment technology to the former. A. Q. Khan, best known as the "father of Pakistan's nuclear weapons programme", was the key figure in making this exchange happen. His clients included not only North Korea but also Iran and Libya, two other countries in search of their own nuclear weapons (Chinoy 2008). This way, Khan became instrumental in North Korea's development of its HEU programme. China sometimes acted as an intermediary between North Korea and Pakistan, as they traded missiles for nuclear technology (Chinoy 2008). In the meantime, Pyongyang had stopped its missile tests in 1994. But in 1998, it launched an intermediate-range Taepodong-1 missile over the East Sea and Japan. While developing a clandestine HEU programme, North Korea was becoming more open about its development of missiles.

The second North Korean nuclear crisis began in October 2002. As explained in Chapter 3, the George W. Bush administration had become critical of the Agreed Framework, which it thought was too soft on North Korea. After almost two years in office, the administration sent a delegation to North Korea to discuss the country's nuclear programme. On the first day of the meeting, the visiting US delegation confronted their North Korean counterparts with evidence of their country's possession of the HEU programme, which was in contravention of the Agreed Framework. The North Korean side admitted the existence of the programme, even if the following day it backtracked on its admission (Funabashi 2007). Arguably, Pyongyang was thinking that the Bush administration was starting a new negotiation process similar to that of the Clinton administration during the first nuclear crisis. Alas, this was not the case. The United States effectively terminated the Agreed Framework in December 2002. One month later, North Korea announced that it would withdraw from the NPT. This time, it carried through with its announcement. In April 2003, North Korea left this treaty (IAEA 2023). The United States and North Korea launched the Six-Party Talks together with South Korea, China, Japan and Russia, resulting in the September 2005 Joint Statement of the Fourth Round of the Six-Party Talks. The statement essentially reproduced the denuclearization for diplomatic relations and economic aid deal of the Agreed Framework. But it was a case of too little, too late. North Korea had decided to go nuclear.

North Korea's reasons for becoming a nuclear power even as it negotiated the Six-Party Talks Joint Statement remain unclear, given the opacity of the Kim regime. The rationale described above still applied: the Kim family wanted security and prestige. But there was something more. The United States had invaded Afghanistan in 2001 and Iraq in 2003. Iraq had been included in an "Axis of Evil" that, according to Bush, had links with terrorist groups. Iran and North Korea were the two other countries included in this axis. In the aftermath of the 9/11 terrorist attacks on New York and Washington, DC, from which the invasion of Iraq had followed, Pyongyang could credibly believe that it might be on the receiving end of an invasion or at least a military strike (Howard 2004), particularly since weapons of mass destruction (WMD)-free Iraq did not really have any connection with the 9/11 terrorist attacks and Saddam Hussein's troops had quickly folded following the US-led invasion. It should be said that North Korea also ended up using its nuclear programme as a source of revenue, exporting technology and expertise to third countries (see below).

North Korea, therefore, conducted its first nuclear test on 9 October 2006. With an estimated yield of a maximum two kilotons, the test was not particularly powerful. But then, only seven countries had conducted nuclear tests before North Korea: the United States, the Soviet Union, the United Kingdom, France, China, India and Pakistan; Israel had never conducted an actual test, as far as is known. This was a very selective list to be part of. North Korea celebrated accordingly, and would go on to conduct further tests in May 2009, still under Kim Jong-il, February 2013, January and September 2016, and September 2017, in these last four cases under Kim Jong-un. The most recent test had a yield of up to 280 kilotons (CSIS 2022).

At the same time, North Korea also accelerated development of its missile programme. Kim Jong-il resumed missile testing from 2003 to

2009, including both short-range and intermediate-range missiles. But it was Kim Jong-un who took the North Korean missile testing programme to new heights. From 2012 onwards, he conducted a record number of missile tests, including Pyongyang's first intercontinental ballistic missile (ICBM) tests in 2017. In a period of only five years between 2012 and 2017, Kim ordered more missile tests to take place than his father and grandfather had in the period between 1984 and 2009. In 2022, North Korea conducted more than double the number of tests of any previous year (CSIS 2022). By 2023, North Korea had a sophisticated nuclear and missile arsenal, with some sources venturing that the Kim family was in possession of up to 115 nuclear warheads (Kim & Kim 2023). Plus, in September 2023 North Korea unveiled its first tactical nuclear attack submarine (Smith & Choi 2023). In case of war, South Korea and the United States would have to contend not only with a potential nuclear strike from North Korean territory but also from a potential underwater nuclear launch.

In conversations with multiple North Korean officials over a period of more than a decade, it has become apparent that Pyongyang has no intention of giving up its nuclear weapons. To the examples of Afghanistan and Iraq cited above, many North Koreans also add the case of the forceful removal of power of Gaddafi in 2011 after he decided to give up Libya's WMD, as well as Russia's invasion of Crimea, in 2014, and attempted invasion of the whole of Ukraine, in 2022, as other examples of why the possession of nuclear weapons matters for smaller powers. The example of Gaddafi is particularly enlightening from a North Korean perspective because, in the view of my interlocutors, the Libyan leader was removed from power thanks to the support that the United States and several European countries gave to rebels fighting his regime, less than a decade after he had voluntarily agreed to relinquish his country's WMD in exchange for normalization of relations with the West. But the example of Crimea and the rest of Ukraine is also instructive for North Korea in that, from the perspective of my interlocutors, Kyiv would have avoided an invasion from Russia had it kept the nuclear weapons remaining in its territory following the disintegration of the Soviet Union.

In fact, conversations with North Koreans about the possibility of denuclearization tend to follow a familiar pattern. North Korean officials argue that they will only give up nuclear weapons if there is a nuclear-free Korean Peninsula. By this they mean not only the removal of US nuclear weapons from South Korea, which already happened in 1991, but also the removal of South Korea from Washington's nuclear umbrella. The latter is very unlikely to happen so long as North Korea possesses nuclear weapons. And even then, South Korea would have an interest to be under the nuclear umbrella of the United States since its (unfriendly) neighbours China and Russia also possess their own nuclear arsenals. In other words, North Koreans are setting conditions that are impossible to meet, thereby indicating that denuclearization is not a realistic proposition.

In this sense, discussions with North Korea about its nuclear programme are essentially an opportunity to hear why Pyongyang does not trust the United States, South Korea or even China and Russia. North Korea feels isolated and threatened both by external forces as well as real or imaginary internal ones. Pyongyang cannot trust Beijing or Moscow to come to its rescue if it is under attack or prey to an internal revolution. Thus, possession of nuclear weapons seems to be the only reason why the Kim regime can metaphorically sleep well at night. Ultimately, nuclear weapons show how isolated Pyongyang feels.

NORTH KOREA AND THE NON-PROLIFERATION REGIME: PYONGYANG'S NUCLEAR LINKS AND IMPACT

North Korea's nuclear programme benefited from the support of the Soviet Union, China and Pakistan. Likewise, North Korea received Chinese and Soviet help when it started to develop its own conventional arms industry in the 1950s, as both Beijing and Moscow transferred technology and know-how (Berger 2016). In the 1970s, Egypt provided North Korea with Soviet Union-designed Scud-B missiles. In other words, and despite claims of self-reliance, North Korea has a long tradition of acquiring foreign technologies and know-how to accelerate development of its nuclear and other weapons. It does not hesitate to reach out to other parties when it feels the need.

Likewise, North Korea has a long history of exporting arms and know-how to third countries and guerrilla and insurgent groups. One of the reasons for engaging in this trade is ideology. Building on its self-identification as an anti-imperialist Third World country involved in the struggle against the United States and its capitalist friends, North Korea sold conventional weapons, munitions and rocket launchers to countries in Africa, Latin America and the Middle East (Young 2021a). From the perspective of Kim Il-sung, arming Third World countries served the greater cause of independently resisting the United States and, to an extent, the Soviet Union as well. In fact, over the decades North Korea has also built arms factories in countries such as the Democratic Republic of Congo, Ethiopia, Madagascar and Yemen that would have allowed these countries to manufacture their own equipment (Berger 2016). And over the decades, the Korean People's Army has trained armed forces and insurgencies in countries such as Benin, the Democratic People's Republic of Congo, Egypt, Libya, Mozambique, Nigeria, the Seychelles, Syria, Uganda and Zimbabwe (Berger 2016). The list of North Korea's clients is long and varied.

The main reason why North Korea sells arms, however, is arguably more prosaic: money. North Korea has few assets or products to export and is not an attractive investment destination. But it has advanced enough weapons and is willing to sell them to the highest bidder, or rather, to any willing customer. Plus, its labour is cheap and for sale, so that the construction and training activities form another source of revenue for Pyongyang's coffers. Most notably, the Middle East became North Korea's main market in the 1980s. With money from oil and gas flowing into several countries in the region and an unstable regional environment, Middle Eastern clients became North Korea's top buyers. Iran and Libya allegedly became the country's main clients, with other countries such as Egypt and Syria also becoming important buyers of North Korean weapons. As North Korea also started to export more expensive armaments, especially missiles, the Middle East became an even more important client given its economic resources. North Korea even built short-range missile factories in countries such as Egypt, Iran, Libya and Syria (Berger 2016). In fact, by the early 1990s North Korea sought to negotiate a deal with Israel whereby Pyongyang would stop its exports to the Middle East in exchange for Israeli investment in its economy (Shai 2016). This offer further underscored the fact that hard cash rather than ideological convergence is the primary motive driving North Korean arms sales.

Throughout the 1990s, as North Korea continued to develop its missile and nuclear programmes, although suffering economically as a result of the end of Soviet and Chinese patronage, the proliferation of WMD became an obvious route for the North Korean regime to attract much-needed capital and to barter for goods such as oil (Cha 2018). The United States, South Korea and their allies and partners were aware of this trade but were unable to stop it. After all, North Korea had decades of experience in exporting arms to third parties. These deals and transfers certainly were not done openly. By the time the international community sought to stop Pyongyang, it was frequently too late.

In May 2003, the George W. Bush administration launched the Proliferation Security Initiative (PSI). Concerned about the failure of the non-proliferation regime to stop North Korean exports of nuclear technology and missiles, the United States launched the PSI to interdict shipments going from Pyongyang to third parties. Washington's Asian and European allies and partners signed up, as did some countries in Africa and the Americas (US Department of State 2023). The initiative scored some victories, such as the interdiction of missile shipments to Yemen (Doolin 2006). Yet the PSI was unable to completely stop North Korea's trade and bartering of its missiles and nuclear technology. After all, there is a confluence of interests between a North Korea seeking cash or products and its clients seeking to upgrade their military capabilities.

Iran is probably North Korea's best-known and most reliable partner. Dating back to the Iranian Revolution of 1979, Tehran has been engaged in an ideological confrontation with Washington. Arguably, Iran and the United States have also been engaged in a decades-old proxy war, given Tehran's support for regimes and groups opposing Washington's allies such as Israel and Saudi Arabia. And with Iran fighting a war of its own against Iraq during 1980–88, North Korea seized the opportunity and started to sell weapons to the Iranian regime a few months after the revolution that brought it to power, eventually including missiles (Berger 2016). Pyongyang quickly gained a reputation as a reliable and relatively low-cost provider of weapons.

Throughout the 1990s, Iran sought to upgrade its military capabilities and became one of North Korea's most important missile and nuclear clients (Fitzpatrick 2006). As any salesperson knows, nothing beats a product demonstration. By attending North Korea's tests, Iranian officials and scientists could see first-hand the preparations that North Korea takes before a test as well as the test itself. This way, North Korea has been able to build an enduring trade relationship with Iran.

With regard to Iran's own nuclear ambitions, Israel's possession of nuclear weapons and competition with Saudi Arabia are the main reasons why the current Iranian regime wants to develop nuclear weapons for itself. Paradoxically, Iran's nuclear programme can be traced back to the 1950s, when it received support from the United States to build its programme for peaceful purposes such as electricity generation (Patrikarakos 2012). However, the 1979 revolution and immediate breakdown in relations with the United States and enmity with Israel resulted in Iran developing a clandestine nuclear weapons programme, which is where North Korea fits in. North Korean and Iranian scientists have been cooperating with each other, Pyongyang has transferred technology such as nuclear centrifuges to Iran and North Korean experts have been involved in the design of Iranian nuclear reactors (Fitzpatrick 2006).

In fact, the North Korean and Iranian nuclear crises became intertwined throughout the 2000s. To begin with, the two countries were part of Bush's original "Axis of Evil". Furthermore, in the early 2000s there were reports that Iran was developing a clandestine uranium enrichment programme, much like North Korea. In 2005, the UN, the United States and the EU started to impose sanctions on Iran after the IAEA found that Iran was non-compliant with its safeguards agreement. This did not stop Iran's nuclear programme, as the country opened its first nuclear reactor in 2011 (Patrikarakos 2012). Later on, the P5+1 group – comprising the UN Security Council's five permanent members (China, France, Russia, the United Kingdom and the United States) plus Germany – and the EU, launched negotiations with Iran. Tehran, on the one hand, and the P5+1 and the EU, on the other, reached an agreement in July 2015, but then Donald Trump withdrew the United States from it on taking office. This allowed Tehran to further develop its nuclear programme, even if ever stronger sanctions, particularly from the United States and the EU, made it more costly for the Iranian regime to pursue its nuclear weapons programme. At the time of writing, in early 2024, negotiations with Iran are ongoing, having resumed once Joe Biden became the US president in 2021 (Brewer & Rome 2023). Iran's nuclear programme is certainly less developed than North Korea's, with the country not being in possession of any nuclear weapon as of early 2024. But the pattern of negotiations, agreement and breakdown of the agreement has parallels with the case of North Korea. And with Pyongyang having supported Tehran's development of its nuclear programme, North Korea is not only an example for Iran, thanks to its successful development of nuclear weapons, but also a direct contributor to the crisis between Tehran and the countries that want to stop the programme.

Syria is arguably North Korea's next closest partner when it comes to proliferation activities by the Kim regime. Hafez al-Assad, the father of current leader Bashar al-Assad, initiated a coup in 1970, and Syria's relationship with North Korea followed a similar pattern to Iran's. Starting in the 1970s, North Korea started to sell arms to a Syria engaged in conflicts with Israel and the Lebanon War of 1982. From the late 1980s onwards, Syria started to purchase North Korean missiles as well, thus upgrading their military relationship (Berger 2016). From the beginning, the al-Assad family came to see the Kims as reliable partners.

Focusing on nuclear cooperation between the two countries, Syria's nuclear programme can be traced back to the 1960s and to the years before the al-Assad family seized power. Israel's possession of a nuclear weapons programme and its rapid victory during the Six-Day War of 1967, when Syria was defeated along with Egypt and Jordan, convinced Syrian leaders that they needed their own deterrent. Initially, they settled for chemical weapons, also with the support of North Korea as well as countries such as Egypt and the Soviet Union. By the 1990s, Hafez al-Assad decided to also develop a nuclear weapons programme (Feldman 1997). After all, Syria continued to have an adversarial relationship with Israel and the United States.

North Korea quickly became central to Syria's nuclear ambitions. There is evidence that by the mid to late 1990s Pyongyang was helping Damascus build a nuclear reactor following the specifications of its Yongbyon facility. Bashar al-Assad then became Syria's president in 2000, following the death of his father. The new Syrian leader accelerated development of the country's nuclear programme, with North Korean officials increasing the number of their visits and growing numbers of the country's scientists being dispatched to the Middle Eastern country.

This alarmed American and Israeli intelligence services. In August 2007, Israeli commandos were able to access the (still suspected) nuclear facility and brought back material to their country. They were able to confirm that there were North Korean nuclear materials in the facility. In September, Israel launched Operation Outside the Box. A group of Israeli fighter jets entered Syrian air space, bombed the nuclear reactor to obliterate it, and returned back to Israel (Katz 2019). Photographs released after the attack indeed revealed that the destroyed nuclear reactor had a similar design to Yongbyon. It was the clearest evidence to the rest of the world of the nuclear cooperation between North Korea and a Middle Eastern partner.

Syria was one of the countries most affected by the Arab Spring, starting in late 2010. Even though the al-Assad family retained power, the country was embroiled in a civil war from 2011 that arguably is ongoing as of 2024 – even if the peak in violence finished around 2017. In this environment, and even without considering its own transition in power from Kim Jong-il to Kim Jong-un, it would have been difficult for North Korea to continue to support Syria's nuclear programme. But it would not be unthinkable that, once Bashir al-Assad is once again completely safe in power, nuclear cooperation between North Korea and his regime will resume.

Then there is the case of Pakistan. On this occasion, North Korea was on the receiving end of support with its nuclear programme, as noted above. But at the same time, Pyongyang provided missile technology, components and know-how in return (Berger 2016). This increased the nuclear threat coming from Pakistan, since potentially it could use the missiles that North Korea has transferred to allow it to develop the capability to mount a nuclear warhead and launch a strike. This explains why the relationship between North Korea and Pakistan was and remains of great concern to the United States and its allies.

There are also suspicions that North Korea may have supported Myanmar's incipient nuclear programme in the early 2000s, but there is no conclusive proof that this has been the case. Likewise, in the past there were unconfirmed rumours that North Korea supported Muammar Gaddafi's nuclear programme in the 1990s and early 2000s, when the former Libyan leader was seeking nuclear weapons capability. Similarly, Egypt's flirtation with the development of nuclear weapons and longstanding arms purchases from North Korea, including missiles, has raised fears that Pyongyang and Cairo would be tempted to forge a partnership in this area, despite Egypt's generally positive relations with the United States (Berger 2016; Pollack 2011). The point is that would-be nuclear powers are aware that North Korea's nuclear materials and know-how are up for sale. If the client pays the right price, the Kim family is willing to sell its nuclear secrets.

More generally, North Korea is arguably the greatest threat to the nuclear non-proliferation regime. According to the NPT, there are five recognized nuclear weapon states: China, France, Russia, the United Kingdom and the United States. This may seem unfair to other would-be nuclear weapon states, but it is generally accepted by the international community. There are also three countries that are non-parties to the NPT: India, Israel and Pakistan. Unsurprisingly, these are the three other countries in possession of nuclear weapons. Technically, therefore, none of them has breached the terms of the NPT since they never joined the treaty to begin with. (South Sudan, established in 2011 and the last country to join the UN, is yet to sign the NPT as well.)

This leaves North Korea in a group of one: the only country to join the NPT, start development of its nuclear weapons programme in earnest, withdraw from the NPT, and conduct a nuclear test and develop its nuclear arsenal. Article X of the treaty allows for a party to withdraw "if it decides that extraordinary events, related to the subject matter of this Treaty, have jeopardized the supreme interests of its country".[2] It is generally accepted that North Korea did not meet this condition when it decided to withdraw from the NPT in 2003. In other words, North Korea disregarded the terms of the treaty it had signed up to because it was an unnecessary hindrance to its development of an autonomous nuclear programme.

North Korea has therefore set a precedent that other countries could follow. Take the case of countries in the Middle East, several of which have pursued or remain actively pursuing nuclear weapons of their own. They could decide that adherence to the NPT is a formality they can dispense with, since they feel threatened by Israel's nuclear programme and it is widely known that they have nuclear ambitions. Therefore,

2 Treaty on the Non-Proliferation of Nuclear Weapons. 1 July 1968.

they could follow in the steps of North Korea and technically be free to pursue a nuclear weapons programme. After all, UN sanctions on North Korea only started to be implemented from 2006 and they were related to its nuclear and missile tests. They were not related to withdrawal from the NPT per se.

Or take the case of North Korea's neighbours, Japan and South Korea. It is widely acknowledged that both could develop nuclear weapons in a relatively short period of time, since they possess the necessary expertise and materials to build their own arsenals. Both countries can credibly argue that they feel threatened by North Korea's nuclear weapons programme, given that the country regularly conducts missile tests that directly threaten both of them. In the case of South Korea, North Korea has explicitly stated that its nuclear programme targets the country and has even modelled strikes on it (Shin 2023b). With doubts about the USA's nuclear umbrella mounting following the Trump presidency, and wary of North Korea's own nuclear developments, around two-thirds of South Koreans favour development of their own country's nuclear weapons (Pacheco Pardo 2023b). Considering the examples of India and Israel, there is a distinct possibility that South Korea could build its own nuclear arsenal without suffering major economic or political consequences.

In addition, North Korea threatens the nuclear non-proliferation regime because it has proved that sanctions do not work. Iran, Syria or any other would-be nuclear powers can credibly believe that they will be able to build their nuclear arsenal even if the UN, United States and EU impose sanctions. In fact, the main rationale behind the P5+1 negotiations with Iran was to find a diplomatic solution to the regime's nuclear ambitions before its programme became irreversible. Supporters of negotiations with Tehran argue that this is their best chance to stop Iran (Brewer & Rome 2023). In the case of Syria, Israel's 2008 military strike was essentially the result of a belief by Israeli leaders that they had to look after their country themselves (Katz 2019). That is, Israel did not think that negotiations with the al-Assad regime could lead to denuclearization. And they had the recent example of the failed Six-Party Talks involving North Korea to back that view.

In short, North Korea is a "bad" example for countries and policymakers, who believe that international regimes and international law should govern international relations and global politics. The non-proliferation regime has been a pillar of the Liberal International Order (LIO) for decades. This order is now challenged by China, Russia and North Korea itself, as well as by the many countries outside the West that think that the order is a US-led system that does not necessarily suit them. North Korea proves to critics of the LIO that they can go against it, even in such a fundamental issue as the (non-)development of nuclear weapons.

UNACCEPTABLE BUT ACCEPTED? THE INTERNATIONAL COMMUNITY AND NORTH KOREA'S NUKES

South Korea, the United States and the international community at large have no intention of accepting North Korea's status as a nuclear weapons state. But the reality is that this same international community has to deal with a nuclear North Korea. And a nuclear North Korea poses a direct threat to the foundations of the LIO that was founded towards the end of the Second World War with the establishment of the UN, the IMF and the World Bank. Throughout the Cold War, this US-led order was in competition with the Soviet-led communist bloc, which it was able to "defeat" in 1991 when the Soviet Union collapsed. This set the conditions for the strengthening of what thus became a global order with the United States as the hegemonic power. The UN-approved military intervention to support Kuwait after its invasion by Iraq in 1991 and the launch of the World Trade Organization (WTO) in 1995 epitomized the global nature of the liberal order. Back in the 1990s it seemed as if this order was accepted by countries around the world.

Yet North Korea's 2006 nuclear test was one of the signs that the order was not universal after all. For the test and subsequent nuclear status of North Korea undermined one of the bases of the liberal order: the non-proliferation regime. Other signs were the return of the use of war by great powers to effect change in smaller powers, such as the cases of the United States with Iraq or Russia with Ukraine; the Global Financial Crisis (GFC) of 2008 that crudely reflected some of the negative effects of economic globalization; and the paralysis of institutions such as the UN and the WTO. Thus, North Korea's nuclear programme has to be placed in the context of a broader weakening of the LIO throughout the first three decades of the twenty-first century. This helps inform the response to North Korea's nuclear programme by third countries and institutions.

Furthermore, North Korea's nuclearization also needs to be placed in the context of the rise of so-called illiberal regimes, which are not only dissatisfied with the LIO as currently structured but would also like to replace it. These regimes want new rules to play the international politics game. China is the best-known and most powerful case of an illiberal regime seeking to bend the international system to accommodate its own characteristics. Other prominent examples include countries such as Iran and Russia, as well as countries with imperfect democracies, including India and Turkey (Economist Intelligence Unit 2023). North Korea is among the authoritarian regimes dissatisfied with the liberal order that would like to replace it with a different international system. In fact, North Korea has strong links with China in particular, Russia and, to an extent, Iran, as shown throughout this book. These links also help inform the ways in which different countries have responded to Pyongyang's nuclearization.

The United States has been at the forefront of efforts to stop North Korea's nuclear programme. Throughout the 1990s, the Clinton administration took an approach based on negotiations and economic incentives. Throughout the first nuclear crisis of 1993–4, US officials approached negotiations with their North Korean counterparts based on the principle that Washington had to move the Kim regime into a position where it felt that it would be rewarded for ending its nuclear ambitions (Wit, Poneman & Gallucci 2004). The Agreed Framework reflected this approach. North Korea was given clear and specific economic benefits in exchange for an end to its nuclear programme, as well as the promise of further economic benefits derived from potential integration in the world economy, together with political benefits, most notably diplomatic normalization with Washington.

The launch of KEDO in 1995 reflected this quid pro quo. The United States led an international consortium to build two light water reactors that would provide North Korea with the energy-generation capacity that it was losing by giving up its "civilian" nuclear programme (KEDO 2024). South Korea, Japan and the European Union were among the countries and institutions contributing to KEDO, proving both the position of the United States as the leader of the LIO at the time but also their own belief in engagement and incentives as the way to make the Kim family give up its nuclear ambitions. The United States also provided economic aid to North Korea for the first time during the great famine of the mid-1990s (World Food Programme 2023b). This gesture indicated that Washington had no problems with the North Korean population. Rather, it was the Kim family's nuclear programme that was the issue. As explained previously, towards the end of the Clinton administration, the president even considered the possibility of normalizing diplomatic relations with North Korea (Clinton 2004). Clinton could not carry through with his plan as other foreign policy issues demanded his attention towards the end of his presidency. But his willingness to entertain this idea demonstrated that engagement was part of the US approach towards North Korea.

At the same time, the United States also started to make clear that sanctions and pressure were part of its toolkit to deal with North Korea's nuclear programme. Throughout the 1990s, Washington imposed sanctions on Iran, Libya, Syria and Pakistan in relation to their military links with North Korea, sending a clear message to Pyongyang.[3] Plus, the Republican Party-dominated US Congress refused to free the necessary funding for the United States to contribute to the building of KEDO as promised (Wit, Poneman & Gallucci 2004). This showed that there were US policy-makers who thought that the United State was giving away too much to North Korea, in exchange for what many believed was simply an incipient and underdeveloped nuclear programme. It was a trade-off that many in the United States were not willing to make.

The 1990s started to saw the political rise of China at the global level, coming on the heels of its rapid and impressive economic development. As North Korea's treaty ally, border-sharing neighbour and economic lifeline throughout the decades, China plays a special role in discussions about the denuclearization of North Korea. To put it in simple terms, China is opposed to a nuclear North Korea because this creates instability in Northeast Asia. At the same time, Beijing is generally comfortable

3 See US Department of the Treasury 2023. "Sanctions List Search Tool". https://ofac.treasury.gov/sanctions-list-search-tool.

with having North Korea as a buffer state between US forces stationed in South Korea and its own territory (Chen 2023). Chinese leaders, therefore, value the benefits of a nuclear-armed yet safe and stable North Korea over the potential yet unproven benefits of a nuclear-free yet unsafe North Korea.

China's first direct encounter with the political effects of North Korea's nuclear programme was during the Four-Party Talks of 1997–8. The United States, as well as South Korea, felt that it was necessary to involve the Jiang Zemin government in one of the key security dilemmas across East Asia. Plus, Washington was involved in a process of the so-called socialization of Beijing whereby it was seeking to help integrate China into the LIO and existing international institutions (Johnston 2007). As a result, the North Korean nuclear programme and the way that the United States and China try to manage its fallout became part of the broader Sino–American relationship. This continues to be the case more than 25 years after the launch of the Four-Party Talks. Participants at the four-way talks, however, would later tell me that China took a backseat while the other three parties led discussions. After all, this was a new format for Beijing to deal with a security conundrum. Nonetheless, Beijing had demonstrated that it should not be left out of negotiations about Pyongyang's nuclear programme.

Inaugurated in 2001, the Bush administration eventually continued the blueprint initiated by the Clinton administration, with two crucial changes. To begin with, economic and diplomatic benefits for North Korea would only come after it had clearly shown that it had stopped development of its nuclear programme. Therefore, the Bush administration terminated KEDO after it found out that North Korea had continued to pursue it. In addition, North Korea's nuclear programme would be part of a broader process dealing with other matters, most notably the Kim family's human rights abuses of the North Korean population. Thus, the United States adopted the North Korea Human Rights Act in 2004, named a Special Envoy for North Korea Human Rights and worked actively so that the UN would issue a condemnation of Pyongyang's human rights record on an annual basis (Howe 2006).

The Six-Party Talks launched in 2003 were also part of Washington's new approach towards North Korea. The idea that the United States had was to multilateralize negotiations about North Korea's nuclear programme so that multiple parties would feel ownership of the process, and also to prevent Pyongyang driving a wedge between Washington and its allies, particularly Seoul. The United States also wanted to continue to involve China in the resolution of the North Korean nuclear conundrum. In fact, Beijing was the host of the talks. This was the first time that China had led multilateral negotiations to address a security issue. By all accounts, the Hu Jintao government did a good job and acted as an honest broker beyond its own self-interests (Funabashi 2007; Pacheco Pardo 2019). From a purely diplomatic point of view, the talks were a success for China.

The Six-Party process also brought two new players into negotiations over North Korea's nuclear programme: Japan and Russia. In the case of Tokyo, Koizumi had met with Kim Jong-il in September 2002. Japan felt directly threatened by Pyongyang's nuclear and missile programme after it had shot a missile over its territory in 1998. Plus, Japan had long been committed to the NPT regime consequent to being the only country in history to have suffered nuclear strikes (Mochizuki 2007). So Koizumi, and subsequent prime ministers, wanted Japan involved. As for Russia, its new president, Vladimir Putin, wanted Moscow to recover from what he saw as the political and economic humiliation of the final Soviet years and the Boris Yeltsin presidency. Putin regarded involvement in Northeast Asian security affairs as an opportunity to diversify Russia's links away from Europe and the post-Soviet space, as well as a chance to showcase Moscow's return to greatness on a global scale. Participation in the possible resolution of the North Korean nuclear conundrum thus came at the perfect time for Putin (Pacheco Pardo 2019). In fact, the new Russian leader had already met with Kim Jong-il in 2000 and marked out a role for his country to play in the Korean Peninsula.

But if there is something that defines the way in which the Bush administration and subsequent American governments have dealt with North Korea, it is sanctions. Following North Korea's missile and, especially, nuclear tests in 2006, the United States started to lead a process whereby the UN Security Council would respond to North Korean nuclear and some egregious missile tests with new rounds of sanctions (UN Security Council 2023b). Interestingly, China and Russia went along with their imposition. As members of the UN Security Council, they could have exercised their veto power and prevented the imposition of multiple rounds of sanctions. But Beijing and Moscow felt that North Korea's actions warranted a political and diplomatic signal (Pacheco Pardo 2019). Yet both countries also blamed the United States for its alleged intransigence towards North Korea and were only half-heartedly committed to the actual implementation of sanctions at best (Arnold 2022; Nichols 2023). This explains why, from 2006 onwards, the United States and other actors, such as the European Union, have also imposed their own autonomous sanctions on North Korea going beyond those of the UN Security Council. In addition, Washington continued to impose sanctions on countries benefiting from North Korea's nuclear and missile programme, particularly in the Middle East.[4] Sanctions were meant to provide an economic hit to the North Korean economy, pressuring the Kim regime to decide that it would be preferable to trade off its nuclear programme in exchange for economic relations with the United States.

Coming to office in 2009, the Obama administration also followed the blueprint established by Clinton to deal with North Korea. This was illustrated by the Leap Day agreement that the United States and North Korea reached in 2012, shortly after Kim Jong-un took office. Once again, both sides agreed that the United States would offer political and economic incentives to North Korea in exchange for denuclearization (Nuland 2012). However, the Obama years were arguably best marked by the United States unofficially acknowledging that the North Korean nuclear issue was becoming irresolvable. Officially, Washington insisted that Pyongyang had to give up all its nuclear weapons and dismantle its nuclear facilities. In private, many officials I had the chance to talk to conceded that North Korea was very unlikely to ever agree to full denuclearization. Thus, the United States started to move towards a position of managing the North Korean nuclear threat, as opposed to solving it. Launching an approach labelled "strategic patience", the Obama administration indicated that negotiations with North Korea would only take place if Pyongyang agreed to denuclearize, while continuing to impose new sanctions on Pyongyang, naming its own Special Envoy for North Korean Human Rights and working together with others in the UN to condemn the Kim family's human rights record (Delury 2013). Arguably,

4 *Ibid.*

this was a time in which a growing number of American policy-makers started to quietly leave aside the North Korean nuclear issue as they focused on more pressing foreign and security policy matters, such as competition with China, growing tensions with Russia and instability in the Middle East. In short, many in the United States felt that North Korea was a secondary foreign policy and security issue.

In the case of China, Xi Jinping's accession to power in 2013 also marked a shift in Beijing's approach towards the North Korean nuclear issue. Pyongyang's 2006 and subsequent nuclear tests and the collapse of the Six-Party Talks were arguably a stain on Chinese diplomacy. As the talks produced agreements, Beijing appeared an apt convenor. Once the agreements were essentially ignored by Pyongyang, the perception of Beijing as a host started to shift. North Korea had shown that it could go against the requests of its patron and even defy its wishes for a nuclear-free Korean Peninsula. The Xi government did call for the resumption of the Six-Party Talks, argued that the United States was as much to blame as North Korea for the latter's nuclear programme and engaged in discussions with Washington and others regarding the programme (Xinhua 2012). At the same time, China would continue to allow UN Security Council resolutions imposing new rounds of sanctions on North Korea to be passed (UN Security Council 2023b). And very pointedly, Xi became the first Chinese president to visit South Korea before meeting with his counterpart in the North. In fact, Xi would not meet with Kim Jong-un during his first five years in office. Similarly to the United States, China essentially put the North Korean nuclear issue aside as it concentrated on other, more pressing foreign policy matters, such as competition with Washington, the Belt and Road Initiative to deepen trade and investment links with third countries and, more broadly, China's ascent to the centre of global politics.

Sensing the change in the mood music coming from the United States and North Korea, Japan and Russia also deprioritized the North Korean nuclear issue. In the case of Tokyo, it launched a military build-up and modernization programme ostensibly to protect itself against North Korea. Ultimately, however, this programme had an ulterior, more important motive: for Japan to defend itself against China. For Tokyo came to see China's rise and actions in its neighbourhood as aggressive and as a threat to its own security (Satake & Sahashi 2021). In the case of Russia, meanwhile, Putin deepened ties with Xi and its policy towards East Asia started to focus more on Japan and South Korea. Ultimately, there was little that Russia could do to influence North Korea's nuclear policy. Thus, Moscow focused on energy aid to Pyongyang and potential economic links with North Korea at large when it came to its policy towards the country (Lukin & Zakharova 2018).

Trump's personal diplomacy with Kim Jong-un throughout 2018–19 completely transformed these policies of neglect. After a year of exchanging threats and insults, Trump took the decision to hold a summit with Kim because, deep down, he believed in his own power of persuasion (Woodward 2018). In other words, Trump believed that where diplomacy, economic incentives and sanctions had failed, he could succeed. The Singapore Summit of June 2018 was the apex of Trump's approach towards North Korea, including his famous tête-a-tête with Kim with only their interpreters in attendance. Yet the statement issued by the two parties after the summit also showed how little things had changed since the Clinton years. More than 20 years after Washington and Pyongyang had signed their Agreed Framework, the Singapore statement was based on the same quid pro quo: economic incentives and diplomatic normalization for Pyongyang in exchange for denuclearization.[5] The collapse of the Hanoi Summit of February 2019, in which Trump and Kim should have agreed on a roadmap to implement their Singapore agreement, showed that neither the United States nor North Korea were willing to move away substantially from their official positions, which made resolution of the Pyongyang nuclear issue very difficult, if not impossible. The third meeting between Trump and Kim in the DMZ in June 2019, this time with South Korea's Moon in attendance, did not serve any meaningful purpose in this respect. After this meeting, Trump essentially resorted to the position pursued by his two predecessors: de facto neglect of North Korea. Taking office in January 2021, Joe Biden took the same approach. By then, it was clear that Pyongyang and its nuclear programme did not command the same attention as it had done in the 2000s.

5 Joint Statement of President Donald J. Trump of the United States of America and Chairman Kim Jong Un of the Democratic People's Republic of Korea at the Singapore Summit. Singapore. 12 June 2018.

At the same time, both the Trump and Biden administrations continued Washington's longstanding policy of imposing new rounds of sanctions on North Korea following its nuclear and missile tests. When possible, they worked via the UN Security Council (UN Security Council 2023b), when not, they resorted to unilateral sanctions (US Department of the Treasury 2023). In addition, Biden also included the Kim family's human rights violations in his policy towards North Korea. (In mid-2016, the United States had sanctioned Kim Jong-un himself for these violations.) Most notably, he appointed a new Special Envoy for North Korean Human Rights (Yonhap 2023), after Trump had ignored this issue during his four-year term.

Interestingly, the flurry of inter-Korean and US–North Korea diplomacy throughout 2018–19 led other countries to engage with the North Korean nuclear issue. Kim Jong-un finally visited China to meet with Xi Jinping in March 2018. The Chinese leader wanted to make sure that he would be the first foreign leader Kim met, before his first inter-Korean summit with Moon. Xi and Kim would go on to meet five times in 2018–19, including the Chinese president's first visit to North Korea since taking office in June 2019 (Sun 2023). Putin, meanwhile, would receive Kim in Vladivostok in April 2019. Meanwhile, Japanese prime ministers Abe Shinzo and Kishida Fumio indicated that they were willing to meet with Kim as well, even if such meetings did not take place (Song 2019). In short, once the United States and South Korea signalled that the time for diplomacy with North Korea had arrived, the other countries in the region once again showed interest in seeking to address its nuclear conundrum. The international community may be forced to reluctantly accept that North Korea is a nuclear power. But, ultimately, this same community would like to convince the Kim family to abandon its nuclear programme.

6

North Korea today and tomorrow

Her Name is Kim Ju-ae. Or so we think. She is believed to have been nine or ten years old at the time of her official unveiling to the North Korean population and the outside world in November 2022, but we do not know for sure. Likewise, we are unsure whether she has an older brother and a younger one, only an older brother, or no siblings at all (even if the last option seems unlikely, for North Korean rulers have always had several children each). But such is the secrecy of the Kim family, we do not know basic facts about Kim Jong-un's daughter. For Kim Ju-ae is none other than the fourth generation of the Kim family that the North Korean media has presented to the outside world. Kim Ju-ae's grandfather, Kim Jong-il, was unveiled as the heir to his own father decades because he took power. Kim Jong-un only had the luxury of two years of having his own public agenda for North Koreans to get used to. For many years it seemed that one of his brothers would be his father's heir (see Chapter 2). It seems that Kim Jong-un is following the template of his grandfather, North Korean founder Kim Il-sung, and will spend decades grooming his daughter, Kim Ju-ae, to one day take his place. Or perhaps Kim Ju-ae will not make it to the top after all, as one of the brothers we think she has could well become her father's favourite or the Kim dynasty may collapse. In any case, Kim Jong-un is already laying the groundwork for the Kim family to continue its rule of North Korea for decades to come.

The nature of Kim Ju-ae's unveiling as heir was hardly normal. By showing pictures of her attending an ICBM test together with her father, a clear message was being communicated. The Kim family has skilfully maintained power for 75 years and while there are many reasons why this has been the case, an important one has been the way in which North

Korea has prioritized nuclear weapons and missiles over the well-being of its own population. The symbolism of the Kim family presenting its next generation during a (successful) ICBM test demonstrated the intrinsic link between the Kim family and arguably the country's greatest achievement: its nuclear and missile programme. Kim Jong-un was portrayed as the custodian of North Korea's independence and, from his perspective, prosperity, which one day he will pass on to his daughter. North Koreans might as well accept this state of affairs.

For those of us who follow Korean Peninsula affairs on a daily basis, the unveiling of Kim Ju-ae proved that the Mount Paektu bloodline trumps all other considerations when it comes to power in North Korea, including gender, in spite of the discrimination that ordinary North Korean women suffer. Kim Yo-jong, Kim Jong-un's sister, is already considered to be the North Korean leader's closest confidante (see Chapter 2). Kim Ju-ae has the potential to go one step further and become the leader herself. We should not be surprised if this does not materialize, such is the brutality of North Korean elite politics, including within the Kim family itself. But, likewise, we should not be surprised either if Kim Ju-ae makes it to the top. The Kims are not ready to relinquish control of "their" country.

THE RETURN OF THE ISOLATED "HERMIT KINGDOM"?

Korea used to be known as the "hermit kingdom" back in the nineteenth century. Once Westerners started to have regular contact with the country, they sought to open it up in the way that they had forced China and Japan to do. Korea, however, resisted external pressure longer than its two neighbours, hence the moniker. As China and Japan became better known to the leaders and peoples of other countries, Korea remained less known and even "mysterious". The few books about the country written in English and other European languages helped those who were interested to gain a glimpse into Korea. But the moniker remained, even as Korea did start to open up around the turn of the century.

As of 2024, North Korea can again be considered a "hermit kingdom". When the Covid-19 pandemic started, North Korea was the first country to fully close down its borders, even before China itself (White

2023). The North Korean leadership knew that its medical facilities were inadequate for their country to effectively deal with a pandemic. This also helps to explain why North Korea was the last country to open its borders once the worst of the pandemic was over. As of early 2024, the Kim regime was yet to fully reopen its border with China and Russia, never mind restarting flights to and from the country. Plus, most foreigners have left the country. Aid workers and most diplomats, the bulk of the foreign population in North Korea, left during 2020–21 as North Korea imposed increasingly harsh restrictions on people's lives because of the pandemic (Mao 2022). They are yet to return at the time of writing. Tourism, meanwhile, has remained off-limits since the start of the Covid-19 pandemic. As of early 2024, it seemed that North Korea was just starting to tentatively open to Russian and Chinese tourists. Not that the Kim regime seems particularly bothered by the absence of so many foreigners from his country, particularly Westerners.

What is more, the Kim regime has taken advantage of the Covid-19 pandemic to seal its border with China. Previously the main route for trade with the outside world, particularly for goods sold in the country's *jangmadang*, and also the main escape route for North Korean defectors, North Korea has erected a wall controlled by guards and cameras (Smith & Kiyada 2023). This way, the North Korean regime is better able to control who crosses the border and what goods make their way in and out of the country. Rather than moving in the direction of tentative opening up and a modest removal of restrictions on the population, as previous market reforms and the 2018–19 inter-Korean and US–North Korea summits seemed to suggest, it seems now as if the Kim family wants to tighten its grip over the North Korean population and economy. Arguably, North Korea's external borders are better sealed in 2024 than they have been at any point since the end of the Cold War.

Plus, it should be remembered that *Juche* continues to be North Korea's guiding ideology, at least in principle. But even if it can be dismissed as a historical relic that never applied in practice to begin with, the official media's daily references to *Juche* imply that at the very least the Kim regime believes that it should pay lip service to this idea. Arguably, the Covid-19 pandemic has given North Korea a real taste of what *Juche* means in practice, as trade with China and Russia ground to a halt after North Korea closed its borders. In fact, even Kim Jong-un felt compelled to acknowledge the dire food situation in the country only a few months into the pandemic (BBC 2021). Since reportedly even the North Korean capital of Pyongyang suffered shortages, even though it has always been better served than the rest of the country, it is not unthinkable that the pandemic caused hunger in different regions where people may find it more difficult to grow their own food. In fact, some media reports suggest that this may have indeed been the case (Ji 2023).

But if North Korea has sometimes been referred to as a hermit kingdom, the reason has been the limited scope of its foreign relations. North Korea is not completely isolated and has different types of relationships and arrangements with other countries. But it is also true that North Korea has few embassies overseas and, likewise, that few countries have a diplomatic presence in Pyongyang, a diplomatic presence that has suffered because of the Covid-19 pandemic. Having spoken to several foreign diplomats and aid workers who have spent time in Pyongyang over the past decade, most if not all of them report that it is one of the most difficult postings because of the isolation of the country. It is unlikely that countries will rush to reopen their embassies in the North Korean capital when permitted. Similarly, North Korean diplomats living overseas have not rotated since the onset of the pandemic (White 2023). This means that they do not necessarily know the reality of what is going on in Pyongyang, since the North Korean foreign service is more opaque than its counterparts in most other countries. North Korean diplomats, therefore, cannot effectively perform their duties in terms of exchange of information with their counterparts in other countries, further embedding the sense of isolation. This was further reinforced by North Korea closing several of its embassies across Africa, Asia and Europe in late 2023 (Shin 2023a).

Sanctions have also contributed to the growing isolation. Sanctions by the UN, the United States and the European Union now target most sectors of the country's economy and certainly go beyond the North Korean WMD programme. There are credible reports that they have had a negative impact on the well-being of ordinary North Koreans, because of fewer goods being sold in the *jangmadang* and the correspondent price increases (Chae 2023b). But sanctions on North Korea are not going to be removed any time soon. Certainly, the United States sees no reason to dispense with them, given that the Kim regime has given no indication that it may consider shifting its stance on its possession of nuclear weapons. And in any case, the conditions that North Korea imposed for itself during the Covid-19 pandemic have been likened to the most comprehensive set of sanctions there could be bar a total blockade of the country's economy. Starvation not seen since the Arduous March of the mid-1990s ensued (Yoon 2023). And yet, North Korea has survived. The logical conclusion is that it will not fold to the sanctions regime it is under.

After all, Kim prizes the stability of his regime above everything else. He is willing to impose hardships on the North Korean population that would lead to revolts in other authoritarian regimes. It should be remembered, for example, that the Arab Spring followed a young Tunisian man's protest at the poor economic conditions in his country, rather than any grand ideological gesture. The economic conditions in North Korea are worse than they are in Tunisia. But the Kim regime has been able to avert a similar revolt because of the degree of control over its own population. Kim's recent actions suggest that, if anything, he will look for new ways to maintain this control. The *byungjin* line that Kim presented shortly after replacing his father as the leader of North Korea seems to only focus on the nuclear programme. Arguably, this shift had already started following the failure of the 2019 Hanoi summit, when it became clear that the United States would not remove sanctions unless North Korea took substantial steps in the direction of denuclearization. This reduced the incentives for Kim to prioritize economic reform, since investment into North Korea will remain very limited while sanctions are in place.

This is not to say that in the future North Korea will not make another push to end its isolation. Even if North Korean history teaches us otherwise, there is a lingering hope among many observers of the country that one day it will move in a different direction. After all, China and Vietnam were similarly authoritarian when they launched their respective economic reform processes. They can serve as an example to the Kim family that opening up the economy is not incompatible with a dictator remaining in power. Both China and Vietnam have been presented as examples of the road that North Korea may travel. As unlikely as this seems today, it may well be that one day the Kim family will launch a similar process in their own country.

NORTH KOREA AND THE OUTSIDE WORLD

The year 2023 marked the 70th anniversary of the end of the Korean War. And in many ways, North Korea is yet to move on from the day when it signed the armistice that finished the conflict. To begin with, and most importantly, inter-Korean relations continue to be stuck where they were in the 1950s. Diplomatic, people-to-people and economic exchanges between the two countries have always been relatively small in number, even during the heyday of Seoul's Sunshine Policy when North Korea was in dire need of external support because of the Arduous March. After Moon Jae-in failed to rekindle the links of that era, many South Koreans seem to have given up hope on Kim Jong-un. Certainly, the Yoon Suk-yeol government (in office at the time of writing in 2024) is prioritizing other foreign policy matters such as navigating Sino–American competition or making South Korea a more globally significant country. North Korea matters for Yoon, but he is not losing sleep thinking about ways to improve bilateral relations.

The distancing between the two Koreas has been further exacerbated by the Covid-19 pandemic and Russia's invasion of Ukraine. The former put an end to any type of inter-Korean contact because North Korea closed its border. Ever since then, Pyongyang has refused to respond to Seoul's many offers to engage in talks or to provide aid and other material support (Berlinger & Kwon 2020; Nam 2023). With regard to the latter, Putin's decision to invade Ukraine has pitted the two Koreas against each other in a proxy war. South Korea has been one of the very few countries outside of NATO to decisively condemn Russia's actions, impose sanctions on Moscow, provide non-lethal military equipment and aid directly to Ukraine and provide lethal aid indirectly via countries such as Poland and the United States. In Asia, it has been the only country to do so at the time of writing (Nam 2023). In sharp contrast, North Korea has been one of the only countries in the world to very publicly back Russia's position that it is responding to NATO's expansionism, including in UN votes, and has also transferred military equipment directly to Russia (Kim 2023). The Koreas' diametrically opposed positions on the war in Europe show how far apart they have grown over the decades.

In the case of the United States, North Korea is yet to move away from its position as of 1953. Certainly, there have been multiple attempts over the decades in which Pyongyang has tried to launch a diplomatic normalization process with Washington. Ultimately, however, North Korea is one of the very few countries in the world that has failed to obtain this mark of international recognition. Even China and Vietnam have established diplomatic relations with the United States while maintaining their communist political systems. And arguably, North Korea has failed to normalize relations with the United States because it has decided to prioritize its nuclear weapons programme over those relations (Pacheco Pardo 2021b). The Kim regime feels that it can better guarantee its own security through nuclear bombs rather than good political relations with the United States, which incidentally should also lead to trade and investment links if the experiences of China and Vietnam can serve as a guide.

North Korea's support for China as Sino–American competition intensifies and staunch support for Russia as it continues its invasion of Ukraine have only erected more obstacles for the United States and North Korea to overcome. From an American perspective, North Korea is akin to an appendix of China when it comes to the competition that Washington and Beijing are engaged in. Other countries may have a more nuanced position and be unwilling to choose between the two of them. This, for example, is the position of most if not all countries in Southeast Asia. But North Korea has not acknowledged any nuance. Rather, it has openly sided with China (see below). As for Pyongyang's position on Russia's invasion of Ukraine, its transfers of weapons to the Russian armed forces have taken place in direct defiance of Washington-led sanctions on countries engaged in this very same activity (US Department of the Treasury 2023). Plus, the United States has been the main provider of weapons to Ukraine. Similarly to the case of the two Koreas, arguably the United States and North Korea can be considered to be engaged in a proxy war even when considering their differences in terms of military might.

Conversely, North Korea's relations with China and Russia are arguably at their closest since the end of the Cold War. Starting with China, Beijing's quest for international leadership means that it is looking for as many partners and followers as possible. North Korea is China's only treaty ally, but is also the perfect partner given its economic and political dependence on Beijing. Without China, the North Korean economy would essentially collapse. Even at the height of the Covid-19 pandemic and with North Korea having closed its borders, the Chinese government provided food and aid to the Kim regime (Yoon & Gale 2022). The longer that sanctions on North Korea continue and the longer that Russia is embroiled in its Ukraine quagmire, the more Pyongyang's economic dependence on Beijing will grow. It is a similar case at the UN. Once China decided to stop supporting new rounds of sanctions on North Korea, back in 2018, the UN Security Council became blocked on this issue (UN Security Council 2023b). The backing from China is crucial for North Korea to continue its nuclear and missile development programme without the fear of greater retribution from the international community.

When it comes to Russia, Putin should certainly feel grateful to Kim that he has been one of the few leaders openly supporting his invasion of Ukraine. For example, not even the Chinese government and the vast majority of the country's firms have dared breach the sanctions imposed by the United States in collaboration with the European Union, South Korea and other partners (Demarais 2023). But more broadly, the relationship between Russia and North Korea has become symbiotic. Russia has been providing energy transfers and limited investment to North Korea for decades, while also shielding it at the UN Security Council when necessary (Lukin & Zakharova 2018). This has included oil transfers after the Covid-19 border shutdown (Reuters 2023b). In return, North Korea has been a staunch supporter of Russia's positions in the UN, regarding NATO's expansion or on security matters. Thus, many analysts talk about a China–Russia–North Korea triangle, with China at the top, Russia as the middle power and North Korea as the junior partner (Lee 2022).

One change in North Korea's relations with the outside world derived from the Covid-19 pandemic relates to its proliferation activities. The PSI had been and continues to be successful in limiting North Korea's transfers of nuclear materials and missiles. And the Covid-19 pandemic hit international cargo transportation because of border closures, which also affected North Korea's weapons transfers. This would be particularly the case for materials and weapons to be transferred to the Middle

East, given the distance that they have to travel and the lengths to which North Korea needs to go to disguise its activities.

Yet we should not forget that proliferation continues to be an important revenue raising source for North Korea. As of 2024, the Kim regime arguably raises more money via cybertheft and other cybercrimes. But its proliferation activities also raise tens if not hundreds of millions of US dollars (UN Security Council 2023a). Plus, they have the added advantage of creating stronger bonds with the countries receiving the weapons. As the case of arms transfers to Russia shows, this continues to be an activity that North Korea willingly engages in. Arguably, North Korea sees proliferation also as a way to undermine what it sees as American hegemony. And any activity that undermines the United States is certainly of interest to the Kim regime.

NORTH KOREA'S PAST, PRESENT AND FUTURE

Readers may have noticed three underlying themes underpinning this book's analysis: the Kim family remains firmly in control of North Korea's destiny; North Korea poses a challenge to the LIO that the United States and many other countries hold dear; and the fortunes of South and North Korea have sharply divided over the decades. It is worth now summarizing the key elements of each of these underlying themes, as a way to succinctly lay out the key points presented in the book.

The fact that the Kim family is one of the most successful dynasties of the twentieth and twenty-first centuries is a puzzle. The Kims have not delivered prosperity to their people, many of whom today are aware of how far behind their country is compared to South Korea or even China. This success has multiple reasons. In the past, North Korean leaders used charisma to retain power. Kim Il-sung was a popular leader among North Koreans, regardless of how he may have been perceived outside of the country. Kim Jong-un has sought to recapture some of the charisma that his grandfather brought to the family. In addition, repression has been key to the Kims retaining power for over seven decades. North Korea's concentration camps and purges have been a feature since shortly after the foundation of the country. At the time of writing, ordinary North Koreans still fear being sent to a prison camp in an almost arbitrary manner, whereas elites have to tread carefully to ensure that they do not fall from grace. Plus, North Korea's possession of nuclear weapons has all but ensured that no outside power will seek to remove the Kims from office. Afghanistan, Iraq and Ukraine are cautionary tales from which North Korea has learnt.

The implications of the Kims retaining control over North Korea are profound. To start with, they serve as an example to other dynasties such as the al-Assads in Syria or the Al Saud in Saudi Arabia. These and other families interested in transferring power across generations can look at the example of North Korea to understand how to achieve this feat. Furthermore, the Kims have proved unwilling and unable to seek reconciliation with South Korea, improve relations with the United States, make necessary changes to the North Korean economy, demilitarize society or decisively distance themselves from China to reduce dependence. This suggests that Pyongyang's domestic and foreign policy will continue to be defined by these features. We can argue that this brings stability to North Korean policy. Yet North Korea does not need stability. Rather, it needs to make the necessary changes to improve the living conditions of its own population while also becoming more integrated with other countries across the world.

Moving on to North Korea's challenge to the LIO, this is not to suggest that the order is perfect or that it is not being challenged by other actors. The GFC and global inequality are examples of the shortcomings of the order. And China, Russia, Iran and many others are dissatisfied with this order as it currently stands. Thus, North Korea's stance on the LIO is part of a broader challenge to the United States, South Korea and other countries and institutions supportive of liberalism at the global level. Arguably, it is the area of security where North Korea's challenge to the order is clearest. This obviously relates to its successful development of an advanced nuclear and missile programme, in defiance of the NPT. But North Korea also presents a challenge to UN Security Council sanctions, which are considered a liberal tool to modify the behaviour of third parties without having to resort to violence. And with its support of Chinese and Russian actions, including Putin's decision to invade Ukraine, North Korea is among a set of countries bonding over their displeasure with the US-led liberal order.

The main implication of Pyongyang's challenge to the LIO is that it creates problems for international cooperation, which liberals claim is one of the cornerstones of their preferred order. Take the case of the NPT. Clients of North Korea's nuclear technology and missiles are acting against the interests of those who want international regimes to govern the behaviour of states. Plus, the response to North Korean actions has become divisive. Most notably, sanctions – the liberal tool – are controversial. Many countries have refused to apply them, since they consider North Korea's nuclear programme a problem for the United States and the NPT regime that Washington leads but not to themselves. In addition, North Korea presents an ideological challenge to the liberal order's belief that economic openness and democracy are the natural end point of polities across the world. North Korea clearly defies this idea. It may be poor, but it is living proof that a country can survive with a distinctly illiberal system.

The differences between South and North Korea encompass politics, economics, security and even culture. South Korea is democratic and North Korea authoritarian. South Korea is a market economy and North Korea follows a state-controlled model. South Korea is a key contributor to managing global security issues, from non-proliferation to peacekeeping, and North Korea is a major threat to global security. And South Korea has become the purveyor of Asian culture thanks to *Hallyu* whereas North Korean culture is hardly known beyond the country. Ask people on the street at random and they will probably link South Korea to K-pop or K-dramas, or perhaps semiconductors and mobile phones, and North Korea to nuclear weapons or the Kim family. Their diverging fortunes are the result of the decisions taken by their leaders, along with the behaviour of their peoples. In the 1960s, Park Chung-hee decided that the future of the South Korean economy lay in its integration with global trade and financial flows. In the 1980s, Chun Doo-hwan was forced to accept that dictatorship would need to give way to democracy following mass protests by the South Korean population. In the 1990s, Kim Dae-jung took advantage of the quality of South Korean art to promote *Hallyu* globally. In contrast, Kim Il-sung, Kim Jong-il and Kim Jong-un have focused on their own safety and fortune above everything else, and the North Korean people have been unable to challenge them.

The implication of the stark division between the two Koreas is that reunification and even reconciliation are becoming ever harder to achieve. Most South Koreans still want reunification, according to multiple polls and surveys. But it is not their top priority, and the potential costs of reunification need to be factored in when discussing this matter in the South. As for North Korea, it is (understandably) afraid that reunification is a code word for absorption. When and if reunification comes, South Koreans will not want the North Korean political and economic system in place. North Koreans, meanwhile, are very likely to quickly realize the shortcomings of their model when entering in direct contact with South Korea's. In this context, a key question would be what to do with the Kim family that has ruled North Korea since the beginning. Kim Jong-un himself would not want to find out what the North Korean people would suggest.

In conclusion, North Korea is not an oddity in the twenty-first century. Plenty of other countries and groups pose a challenge to the international system and refuse to accept that the LIO should dominate at the global level. But North Korea is one of the few countries directly and openly challenging the existing world order, whether through the way it governs itself, the way it thinks about itself and others, or the way it conducts itself in the global stage. Those who support the existing world order will have to grapple with the fact that North Korea will continue to challenge their beliefs for the conceivable future.

Bibliography

Arnold, A. 2022. "To sanction North Korea, sanction those that won't – China and Russia". *Bulletin of the Atomic Scientists*, 14 July.

Arnold, G. 2006. *The A to Z of the Non-Aligned Movement and Third World*. Lanham, MD: Rowman & Littlefield.

Balluck, K. 2017. "Trump: North Korea's words, actions 'hostile and dangerous' to US". *The Hill*, 3 September.

BBC 2017. "North Korea nuclear tests: what did they achieve?" BBC, 3 September.

BBC 2021. "Kim Jong-un admits North Korea facing a 'tense' food shortage". BBC, 17 June.

Berger, A. 2016. *Target Markets: North Korea's Military Customers*. Abingdon: Routledge.

Berlinger, J. & J. Kwon 2020. "North Korea isn't talking to the South anymore: experts say it could be trying to manufacture a crisis". CNN, 10 June.

Berlinger, J. & P. Hancocks 2018. "North Korea media praises 'historic' Kim-Moon summit". CNN, 28 April.

Brewer, E. & H. Rome 2023. "Biden's Iran gamble". *Foreign Affairs*, 9 June.

Cha, V. 2018. *The Impossible State: North Korea, Past and Future*. Updated edition. New York: HarperCollins.

Cha, V. & R. Pacheco Pardo 2023. *Korea: A New History of South and North*. New Haven, CT: Yale University Press.

Chae, Y.-h. 2023a. "Kim tells Putin N. Korea supports Russia's 'sacred fight' against West". Yonhap News Agency, 13 September.

Chae, Y.-h. 2023b. "N. Korea's food prices rise, suggesting supply shortages: 38 North". Yonhap News Agency, 24 June.

Chen, Y.-h. 2023. "Lips and teeth: China's buffer thinking toward North Korea". *Journal of Contemporary China*. https://doi.org/10.1080/10670564.2023.2200396.

Chinoy, M. 2008. *Meltdown: The Inside Story of the North Korean Nuclear Crisis*. New York: St. Martin's Press.

Chung, T. 1991. "Korea's Nordpolitik: achievements and prospects". *Asian Perspective* 15(2): 149–78.

Clemens Jr, W. 2010. "North Korea's quests for nuclear weapons: new historical evidence". *Journal of East Asian Studies* 10(1): 127–54.

Clinton, B. 2004. *My Life*. New York: Knopf.

CSIS 2018. "The markets: private economy and capitalism in North Korea". https://beyondparallel.csis.org/markets-private-economy-capitalism-north-korea/.

CSIS 2022. "Missiles of North Korea". https://missilethreat.csis.org/country/dprk/.

Cumings, B. 2005. *Korea's Place in the Sun: A Modern History*. Updated edition. New York: Norton.

Cumings, B. 2010. *The Korean War: A History*. New York: Modern Library.

Delury, J. 2013. "The disappointments of disengagement: assessing Obama's North Korea policy". *Asian Perspective* 37(2): 149–82.

Demarais, A. 2023. "Why China hasn't come to China's rescue". *Foreign Affairs*, 28 April.

Demick, B. 2010. *Nothing to Envy: Real Lives in North Korea*. London: Granta.

Demick, B. 2011. "Some grief over death of North Korea leader false, defectors say". *Los Angeles Times*, 21 December.

Doolin, J. 2006. "The proliferation security initiative: cornerstone of a new international norm". *Naval War College Review* 59(2): 29–57.

Economist Intelligence Unit 2023. *Democracy Index 2022*. London: Economist Intelligence Unit.

Farr, W. 1999. "The Third Temple's Holy of Holies: Israel's nuclear weapons". *The Counterproliferation Papers*. Future Warfare Series No. 2.

Feldman, S. 1997. *Nuclear Weapons and Arms Control in the Middle East*. Cambridge, MA: MIT Press.

Fifield, A. 2016. "North Korea announces five-year economic plan, its first since the 1980s". *Washington Post*, 8 May.

Fifield, A. 2019. *The Great Successor: The Divinely Perfect Destiny of Brilliant Comrade Kim Jong Un*. New York: PublicAffairs.

Fischer, H. 2007. *North Korean Provocative Actions, 1950–2007*. CRS Report for Congress RL30004, 20 April.

Fitzpatrick, M. 2006. "Iran and North Korea: the proliferation nexus". *Survival* 48(1): 61–80.

Funabashi, Y. 2007. *The Peninsula Question: A Chronicle of the Second Korean Nuclear Crisis*. Washington, DC: Brookings Institution Press.

Gumbel, P. 2009. "What Germany got for its $2 trillion". *Time*, 18 May.
Haas, B. & L. Gambino 2018. "North and South Korean leaders meet as US indicates summit may yet happen". *The Guardian*, 27 May.
Han, S. & D. Kim 2022. "North Korea in 2021: Pyongyang's double game". *Asian Survey* 62(1): 53–61.
Heo, U. & T. Roehrig 2018. *The Evolution of the South Korea–United States Alliance*. Cambridge: Cambridge University Press.
Holley, D. 1989. "Pyongyang hosts youth festival: world gets rare peek at N. Korea – and vice versa". *Los Angeles Times*, 29 June.
Horvitz, P. 1993. "U.S. sees 'danger' in North Korean shift". *New York Times*, 15 March.
Howard, P. 2004. "Why not invade North Korea? Threats, language games, and U.S. foreign policy". *International Studies Quarterly* 48(4): 805–28.
Howe, B. 2006. "Strategic implications of the 2004 U.S. North Korea Human Rights Act". *Asian Perspective* 30(1): 191–219.
IAEA 2023. "IAEA and DPRK: chronology of key events". https://www.iaea.org/newscenter/focus/dprk/chronology-of-key-events.
International Institute for Strategic Studies 2023. *The Military Balance 2023*. Abingdon: Routledge.
Ji, D.-g. 2023. "A closer look at North Korea's post-COVID food shortages". *Korea Herald*, 18 April.
Johnston, A. 2007. *Social States: China in International Institutions, 1980–2000*. Princeton, NJ: Princeton University Press.
Katz, Y. 2019. *Shadow Strike: Inside Israel's Secret Mission to Eliminate Syrian Nuclear Power*. New York: St. Martin's Press.
KBS World 2018. "N. Korea's flood relief aid for S. Korea in 1984". http://world.kbs.co.kr/service/contents_view.htm?lang=e&menu_cate=history&id=&board_seq=275253.
KCNA 2011. "UN Human Rights Council urges abrogation of SL". KCNA, 11 June.
KCNA 2013a. "Report on plenary of WPK Committee". KCNA, 31 March.
KCNA 2013b. "S. Korean regime's abuses of human rights condemned". KCNA, 13 December.
KEDO 2024. "Light Water Reactor Project: Overview". http://www.kedo.org/lwr_overview.asp.
Khan, S. 2008. *Nuclear Weapons and Conflict Transformation: The Case of India–Pakistan*. London: Routledge.
Kim, B.-Y. 2017. *Unveiling the North Korean Economy: Collapse and Transition*. Cambridge: Cambridge University Press.

Kim, H. 2018. "End of Korean War might spark end to 'Korea discount' for stocks". Bloomberg, 22 March.

Kim, H. 2023. "Beyond North Korea: possible sources of small arms and light weapons exports to Russia in 2022?" *38 North*, 21 April.

Kim, H.-J. & T.-H. Kim 2023. "Fears, questions about N. Korea's growing nuclear arsenal". *Associated Press*, 22 February.

Kim, I.-s. 1981. "On eliminating dogmatism and formalism and establishing *Juche* in ideological work". In *Kim Il Sung: Works*, Vol. 9, 402–25. Pyongyang: Foreign Languages Publishing House.

Kim, I.-h. 2020. "Ask a North Korean: how restricted is movement in North Korea?" *NK News*, 24 July.

Kim, J. *et al.* 2014. *South Korean Attitudes toward North Korea and Reunification*. Seoul: Asian Institute for Policy Studies.

Kim, K. 2006a. *The Development of Modern South Korea: State Formation, Capitalist Development and National Identity*. London: Routledge.

Kim, N. 2016. *Memory, Reconciliation, and Reunions in South Korea: Crossing the Divide*. Lanham. MD: Lexington Books.

Kim, S. 2006b. *The Two Koreas and the Great Powers*. Cambridge: Cambridge University Press.

Kim, S. & C. Nam 2016. "*Hallyu* revisited: challenges and opportunities for the South Korean tourism". *Asia Pacific Journal of Tourism Research* 21(5): 524–40.

Kim, S.-y. 2024. "N. L. leader calls for defining S. Korea as 'invariable principal enemy' in constitution". *Yonhap News Agency*, 16 January.

Kim, S. & E.-C. Im 2009. "The Kaesong inter-Korean industrial complex: perspectives and prospects". *North Korean Review* 5(2): 81–92.

Kim, W.-h. 2014. *Women of North Korea: A Closer Look at Everyday Life*. Seoul: Institute for Unification Education.

Koh, H. 2000. "A breakthrough in North Korea". *Washington Post*, 2 November.

Korea and World Affairs 1985. "A chronology of U.S. relations with North Korea, 1970–February 1985". *Korea and World Affairs* 9(1): 129–73.

Kramer, C. 1990. "China after Tiananmen Square". *New York Times*, 18 February.

Krishnan, R. 1981. "North Korea and the Non-Aligned Movement". *International Studies* 20(1–2): 299–313.

Kristensen, H. & R. Norris 2017. "A history of US nuclear weapons in South Korea". *Bulletin of the Atomic Scientists* 73(6): 349–57.

Lankov, A. 2002. "Kim takes control: the "great purge" in North Korea, 1956–1960". *Korean Studies* 26(1): 87–119.

Lee, C.-J. 1983. "South Korea in 1983: crisis management and political legitimacy". *Asian Survey* 24(1): 112–21.

Lee, C.-d. 2019. "In DMZ, Trump, Kim agree to resume nuclear talks". *Yonhap News Agency*, 13 June.

Lee, J.-h. 2018. "Hopes for peace after North Korea's Kim Jong-un agrees to shut missile site, visit Seoul". *South China Morning Post*, 19 September.

Lee, J. & W. McKibbin 2018. "Korean unification: economic adjustments under German assumptions". CAMA Working Paper 51/2018.

Lee, N. 2007. *The Making of Minjung: Democracy and the Politics of Representation in South Korea*. Ithaca, NY: Cornell University Press.

Lee, S. 2022. "North Korea is joining China and Russia in confronting the US". *38 North*, 2 March.

Lee, S.-Y. 2023. *The Sister*. London: Palgrave Macmillan.

Lukin, A. & L. Zakharova 2018. "Russia–North Korea economic ties: is there more than meets the eye?" *Orbis* 62(2): 244–61.

Macfie, N. 2010. "Factbox: the battles of the Korean West Sea". Reuters, 29 November.

Mack, A. 1993. "The nuclear crisis on the Korean peninsula". *Asian Survey* 33(4): 339–59.

Maddison Project 2022. Maddison Project Database 2020. https://www.rug.nl/ggdc/historicaldevelopment/maddison/releases/maddison-project-database-2020?lang=en.

Mao, F. 2022. "North Korea: 'first' Covid cases prompt strict national lockdown". BBC, 12 May.

Ministry of Foreign Affairs of the Republic of Korea 2023. "Status of Establishment of Diplomatic Relations". https://www.mofa.go.kr/www/wpge/m_4181/contents.do.

Ministry of Unification of the Republic of Korea 2017. *Understanding North Korea*. Seoul: Ministry of Unification of the Republic of Korea.

Ministry of Unification of the Republic of Korea 2021. *50 Years of Inter-Korean Dialogue*. Seoul: Ministry of Unification of the Republic of Korea.

Ministry of Unification of the Republic of Korea 2023a. "Policy on North Korean defectors". https://www.unikorea.go.kr/eng_unikorea/relations/statistics/defectors/.

Ministry of Unification of the Republic of Korea 2023b. *Report on North Korean Human Rights*. Seoul: Ministry of Unification of the Republic of Korea.

Mobley, R. 2003. *Flash Point North Korea: The Pueblo and EC-121 Crises*. Annapolis, MA: Naval Institute Press.

Mochizuki, M. 2007. "Japan tests the nuclear taboo". *The Nonproliferation Review* 14(2): 303–28.

Mohan, M. 2017. "Rape and no periods in North Korea's army". BBC, 21 November.

Moon, C.-i. 2011. "Between principle and pragmatism: what went wrong with the Lee Myung-bak government's North Korean policy?" *Journal of International and Area Studies* 18(2): 1–22.

Moon, J.-i. 2017. "Address at the Korber Foundation, Germany". 6 July.

Mun, D. 2023. "Daily NK obtains the full text of the Pyongyang Cultural Language Protection Act". *Daily NK*, 23 March.

Nam, H.-W. 2023. "Why is North Korea not responding to inter-Korean military hotline calls?" *Korea Times*, 10 April.

New York Times 1976. "2 Americans slain by North Koreans in clash at DMZ". *New York Times*, 19 August.

Nichols, M. 2023. "US, China, Russia argue over North Korea at United Nations". Reuters, 20 March.

Nicolai da Costa, A. 2018. "What would it take for North Korea to join the IMF?" BBC, 12 October.

Ninkovich, F. 1994. *Modernity and Power: A History of the Domino Theory in the Twentieth Century*. Chicago: University of Chicago Press.

Nixon, R. 1978. *RN: The Memoirs of Richard Nixon*. New York: Simon & Schuster.

Nuland, V. 2012. "U.S.–DPRK bilateral relations". https://2009-2017.state.gov/r/pa/prs/ps/2012/02/184869.htm.

Office of the UN High Commissioner for Human Rights 2023. *Situation of Human Rights in the Democratic People's Republic of Korea: Report of the Special Rapporteur on the Situation of Human Rights in the Democratic People's Republic of Korea, Elizabeth Salmon*. A/HRC/52/65. 9 March.

Oh, K. & R. Hassig 2000. *North Korea through the Looking Glass*. Washington, DC: Brookings Institution Press.

Pacheco Pardo, R. 2013. "Dandong and Sinuiju: the Sino–North Korean border shadow economy". In L. Talani, A. Clarkson & R. Pacheco Pardo (eds), *Dirty Cities: Towards a Political Economy of the Underground in Global Cities*, 89–109. London: Palgrave Macmillan.

Pacheco Pardo, R. 2019. *North Korea–US Relations from Kim Jong Il to Kim Jong Un*. Abingdon: Routledge.

Pacheco Pardo, R. 2021a. "North Korea and the European Union". Oxford Research Encyclopedias. https://doi.org/10.1093/acrefore/9780190228637.013.2042.

Pacheco Pardo, R. 2021b. "Pyongyang's failure: explaining North Korea's inability to normalize diplomatic relations with the United States". *Asia Policy* 16(1): 97–127.

Pacheco Pardo, R. 2022. *Shrimp to Whale: South Korea from the Forgotten War to K-Pop*. London: Hurst.

Pacheco Pardo, R. 2023a. "Historic showmanship between Trump and Kim Jong-un: the possible normalization of US–North Korean summitry". In S. Snyder & K.-A. Park (eds), *North Korea's Foreign Policy: The Kim Jong-un Regime in a Hostile World*, 107–23. Lanham, MD: Rowman & Littlefield.

Pacheco Pardo, R. 2023b. "South Korea could get away with the bomb". *Foreign Policy*, 16 March.

Pacheco Pardo, R. 2023c. *South Korea's Grand Strategy: Making Its Own Destiny*. New York: Columbia University Press.

Pacheco Pardo, R. & S. Kim 2023a. "South Korea: siding with the West and distancing from Russia". *International Politics* 60: 1113–33.

Pacheco Pardo, R. & Y. Kim 2023b. "Russia's invasion of Ukraine and China–North Korea relations: stronger weak–Great Power alignment". *Asian Survey* 62(5–6): 920–44.

Pak, C. 2000. *Korea and the United Nations*. Leiden: Brill.

Pak, J. 2020. *Becoming Kim Jong Un*. New York: Penguin.

Park, C.-h. 1976. *Major Speeches by Korea's Park Chung Hee*. Seoul: Samhwa Publishing.

Park, G.-h. 2013. "Opening a new era of hope". 25 February.

Patrikarakos, D. 2012. *Nuclear Iran: The Birth of an Atomic State*. London: I. B. Tauris.

Plant, T. & B. Rhode 2013. "China, North Korea and the spread of nuclear weapons". *Survival* 55(2): 61–80.

Pollack, J. 2011. *No Exit: North Korea, Nuclear Weapons, and International Security*. London: Routledge.

Potter, W. & A. Stulberg 1990. "The Soviet Union and the spread of ballistic missiles". *Survival* 32(6): 543–57.

Pribbenow, M. 2011. "North Korean pilots in the skies over Vietnam". North Korea International Documentation Project. E-Dossier No. 2.

Reuters 1992. "U.S. and North Korea meet for first cabinet-level talks". *New York Times*, 23 January.

Reuters 2023a. "China's exports to North Korea surge in April". Reuters, 21 May.

Reuters 2023b. "Russia resumes oil exports to North Korea after long pause". Reuters, 14 June.

Roehrig, T. 2017. *Japan, South Korea, and the United States Nuclear Umbrella: Deterrence after the Cold War*. New York: Columbia University Press.

Roh, T.-w. 1988. "A New Era of Reconciliation and Cooperation: Dinner for Prime Minister Lee Kuan Yew of Singapore". 6 July.

Satake, T. & R. Sahashi 2021. "The rise of China and Japan's 'vision' for free and open Indo-Pacific". *Journal of Contemporary China* 30(127): 18–35.

Seth, M. 2018. *North Korea: A History*. London: Palgrave Macmillan.

Shai, A. 2016. "North Korea and Israel: a missed opportunity?" *Israel Journal of Foreign Affairs* 10(1): 59–73.

Shen, Z. (ed.) 2020. *A Short History of Sino–Soviet Relations, 1917–1991*. London: Palgrave Macmillan.

Shin, G.-W. & K. Hwang 2003. *Contentious Kwangju: The May 18 Uprising in Korea's Past and Present*. Lanham. MD: Rowman & Littlefield.

Shin, H. 2023a. "North Korea closes multiple embassies around the world". Reuters, 1 November.

Shin, H. 2023b. "North Korea's Kim oversees simulated nuclear attack against US, South Korea". Reuters, 20 March.

Shiner, J. 1992. "Kim Il-Sung asks for thaw in ties with the U.S.". *Washington Times*, 15 April.

Sims, C. 2000. "North and South Koreans meet on a mountain path". *New York Times*, 15 February.

Smith, J. & S.-H. Choi 2023. "North Korea unveils first tactical, nuclear-armed submarine". Reuters, 8 September.

Smith, J. & S. Kiyada 2023. "North Korea spent the pandemic building a huge border wall". Reuters, 27 May.

Snyder, S. 2018. *South Korea at the Crossroads: Autonomy and Alliance in the Era of Rival Powers*. New York: Columbia University Press.

Song, J.-a. *et al.* 2019. "North Korea touts for investment ahead of Trump–Kim summit". *Financial Times*, 26 February.

Song, S.-h. 2019. "N. K. leader Kim arrives in Vladivostok for summit with Putin". *Yonhap News Agency*, 24 April.

Song, S.-h. 2024. "Russia fired more N. Korean ballistic missiles at Ukraine: White House". *Yonhap News Agency*, 10 January.

Stueck, W. 1997. *The Korean War: An International History*. Princeton, NJ: Princeton University Press.

Suh, D.-S. 1995. *Kim Il Sung: The North Korean Leader*. New York: Columbia University Press.

Suh, D.-S. 2002. "Military-first politics of Kim Jong Il". *Asian Perspective* 26(3): 145–67.

Sun, Y. 2023. "The restoration of special Sino–North Korean relations and Xi Jinping–Kim Jong-un summitry". In S. Snyder & K.-A. Park (eds), *North Korea's Foreign Policy: The Kim Jong-un Regime in a Hostile World*, 87–105. Lanham, MD: Rowman & Littlefield.

Szalontai, B. 2005. *Kim Il Sung in the Khrushchev Era: Soviet–DPRK Relations and the Roots of North Korean Despotism, 1953–1964*. Washington, DC: Woodrow Wilson Center Press.

Takeda, Y. 2006. "Putin's foreign policy toward North Korea". *International Relations of the Asia-Pacific* 6(2): 189–207.

Tertitskiy, F. 2023. *The North Korean Army: History, Structure, Daily Life*. Abingdon: Routledge.

Thae, Y.-h. 2024. *Passcode to the Third Floor: An Insider's Account of Life among North Korea's Political Elite*. Trans. R. Lauler. New York: Columbia University Press.

UN 2022. "General Assembly Resolution demands end to Russian offensive in Ukraine". https://news.un.org/en/story/2022/03/1113152.

UN 2023a. "Member states". https://www.un.org/en/about-us/member-states.

UN 2023b. "UN General Assembly calls for immediate end to war in Ukraine". https://news.un.org/en/story/2023/02/1133847.

UN Human Rights Council 2014. *Report of the Detailed Findings of the Commission of Inquiry on Human Rights in the Democratic People's Republic of Korea*. A/HRC/24/CRP.1, 7 February.

UN Security Council 2023a. "Final Report of the Panel of Experts Submitted Pursuant to Resolution 2627 (2022)". https://daccess-ods.un.org/tmp/486797.839403152.html.

UN Security Council 2023b. "Security Council Committee Established Pursuant to Resolution 1718 (2006)". https://www.un.org/securitycouncil/sanctions/1718.

US Department of State 1998. "Four-Party talks on the Korean peninsula, 1997–98". https://1997-2001.state.gov/regions/eap/korea_4party_talks_1997.html.

US Department of State 2023. "Proliferation Security Initiative". https://www.state.gov/proliferation-security-initiative/#:~:text=Launched%20on%20May%2031%2C%202003,state%20actors%20of%20proliferation%20concern.

US Department of the Treasury 2023. "Sanctions List Search Tool". https://ofac.treasury.gov/sanctions-list-search-tool.

White, E. 2023. "North Korea to restart economic activity after three years of Covid isolation". *Financial Times*, 28 March.

The White House 2002. President Delivers State of the Union Address. https://georgewbush-whitehouse.archives.gov/news/releases/2002/01/20020129-11.html.

Wit, J., D. Poneman & R. Gallucci 2004. *Going Critical: The First North Korean Nuclear Crisis*. Washington, DC: Brookings Institution Press.

Woo, J.-Y. 2016. "South Korean domestic support for the US alliance". *The Asan Forum*. https://theasanforum.org/south-korean-domestic-support-for-the-us-alliance/.

Woodward, B. 2018. *Fear: Trump in the White House*. London: Simon & Schuster.

World Food Programme 2023a. "Democratic People's Republic of Korea". https://www.wfp.org/countries/democratic-peoples-republic-korea.

World Food Programme 2023b. "Food Aid Information System – FAIS". https://www.wfp.org/fais.

Xinhua 2012. "China supports efforts to resume six-party talks". *China Daily*, 23 February.

Yang, M.-s. 2015. *North Korea's Planned Economy and Marketization*. Seoul: Institute for Unification Education.

Yonhap 2018. "N. Korean leader's sister highlights 'charm offensive'". *Yonhap News Agency*, 9 February.

Yonhap 2023. "Biden nominates new special envoy for N. Korean human rights". *Yonhap News Agency*, 24 January.

Yoon, D. 2023. "North Korea suffers one of its worst food shortages in decades". *Wall Street Journal*, 2 March.

Yoon, D. & A. Gale 2022. "North Korea receives aid from China as Covid outbreak spreads". *Wall Street Journal*, 18 May.

Young, B. 2021a. *Guns, Guerrillas, and the Great Leader: North Korea and the Third World*. Stanford, CA: Stanford University Press.

Young, B. 2021b. "Guns in one hand: Kim Jong Un's revitalization of the worker-peasant Red Guards". *NK News*, 17 September.

Index